GUIDE TO THE
ANIMALS
OF SOUTHERN AFRICA

Lynne Matthews

Marius Burger

Acknowledgements

The author wishes to thank the following people and organisations for their help in the preparation of this series:

The Jacana team, for coming up with the idea and making it happen: Jenny Prangley, Megan Mance, Brett Rogers and Shawn Paikin for their resilience and hard work, and Carol Broomhall for her positive stream of feedback and support.

All the incredible photographers who willingly contributed to the project, particularly Marienne de Villiers and the Southern African Reptile Conservation Assessment Group, Jelger Herder, Alan Calenborne, Anna Ekstein and Deon Guyt.

Also thanks to Mandy Brockbank for helping with the additional artwork, Margie Matthews for her incredible and endless supply of help and Greg Matthews for his amazing patience, love and support.

Contents

Mammals

All about mammals 6
The mammals 26
  Cats 26
  Wild dogs 32
  Jackals 33
  Hyenas 34
  Aardwolves 37
  Polecats and badgers 38
  Otters 39
  Civets and genets 40
  Mongooses 41
  Elephants 43
  Rhinos 44
  Hippos 45
  Buffalo 46
  Giraffe 47
  Zebras 48
  Antelope 49
  Hyraxes 57
  Primates 58
  Pigs 60
  Aardvarks and pangolins 61
  Shrews and elephant-shrews 62
  Rabbits and hares 63
  Rodents 64
  Bats 66

Birds

All about birds 70
  Groundbirds 88
  Passerines 94
  Waterbirds 115
  Birds of prey 124
  Scavengers 130

Frogs and Reptiles

All about frogs and reptiles 134
Frogs 152
  Why are frogs different? 152
  Platannas 154
  River frogs 155
  Toads 156
  Sand frogs 157
  Chirping and moss frogs 158
  Rain frogs 159
  Climbing frogs 160
  Dainty frogs 162
  Bullfrogs 163
Reptiles 164
  What are reptiles? 164
  Tortoises and terrapins 165
  The lizard group 171
  Crocodiles 182
  Snakes 184

Insects and other Invertebrates

All about invertebrates 198
The insects 208
  Grasshoppers and crickets 209
  Dragonflies and damselflies 212
  Termites 214
  Antlions 217
  Bugs 218
  Praying mantises 220
  Stick insects 221
  Beetles 222
  Flies and mosquitoes 228
  Ants, bees and wasps 231
  Butterflies and moths 239
Other invertebrates 246
  Snails 247
  Earthworms 248
  Millipedes and centipedes 249
  Spiders 250
  Scorpions 254
  Sun spiders and whip scorpions 257
  Ticks 258

Glossary, References & Index 262

Mammals

▶ All about mammals

Exploring the lives of mammals

Mammals are a popular group of animals. We know far more about them than the other animal groups. But what do you really know about their lives? Have you ever thought how tough it is for them to survive in the wild? Every day they need to find enough food to survive, escape predators that threaten to eat them and compete with other animals for food, space and a mate, which are often in short supply.

This section explores many of the amazing adaptations and habits mammals have developed in order to survive in their environment. There are about 300 species of mammals in southern Africa. We investigate many of them, from the well-known giants, like elephants and giraffes, to ones we see little of and know less about, like molerats and polecats. We have not included any marine mammals in this book.

All mammals have some covering of hair at some stage in their lives, are warm-blooded (or endothermic), and suckle their young on milk produced by the mother.

Rudi Jeggle

Lions may be called 'king of the beasts' but they still have a tough time trying to survive in the wild.

The value of mammals

They are a link in the food chain

A food chain is how all living things depend on each other as food to survive. An example of a very simple food chain is the following: lions eat zebras, which eat grass. These interactions between plants and animals are very important because they help the ecosystem survive.

Herbivores maintain the diversity of plants in a habitat by feeding on them. Without herbivores, a few plant species would take over at the expense of the others.

Carnivores control the numbers of herbivores, which might otherwise destroy the habitat if there were too many of them.

Mammals help others

- Animals that eat fruit and seed pods, like elephants and baboons, help plants by spreading their seeds. The seeds pass through their gut and out onto the ground. The warm, moist dung is an ideal place for seeds to germinate.
- **Dung beetles** depend on dung from mammals for their lifecycle.
- Hyenas clean up the veld by scavenging on dead animals. They prevent the spread of disease.
- Aardvarks, pangolins and **aardwolves** eat thousands of termites every night. Some termites can destroy grasslands and wood used in buildings and houses.

Dung beetles lay their eggs inside the dung balls they roll. The larvae hatch out of the egg and feed on the dung.

The main diet of the aardwolf is harvester termites. Read more about this on page 37.

The science in a name

Every mammal is given its own Latin (or scientific) name and common (or English) name. The Latin name is used all over the world. It is written in italics. Italic letters slope to the right, *like this*. The common name can vary from country to country. Look at the example below.

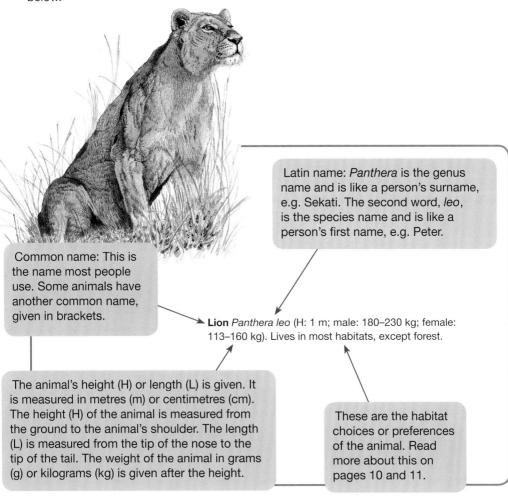

Latin name: *Panthera* is the genus name and is like a person's surname, e.g. Sekati. The second word, *leo*, is the species name and is like a person's first name, e.g. Peter.

Common name: This is the name most people use. Some animals have another common name, given in brackets.

Lion *Panthera leo* (H: 1 m; male: 180–230 kg; female: 113–160 kg). Lives in most habitats, except forest.

The animal's height (H) or length (L) is given. It is measured in metres (m) or centimetres (cm). The height (H) of the animal is measured from the ground to the animal's shoulder. The length (L) is measured from the tip of the nose to the tip of the tail. The weight of the animal in grams (g) or kilograms (kg) is given after the height.

These are the habitat choices or preferences of the animal. Read more about this on pages 10 and 11.

Mammalogy is the study of mammals. A scientist who studies mammals is called a mammalogist. A scientist who studies all animals is called a zoologist.

Classification helps identification

When we classify a mammal, we put it into groups with other animals or mammals that have the same or similar features. **This helps us identify or find out what it is.** Animals in the same group are similar – they are like one another. Animals in different groups are different – they are unlike one another. Examples of group names are Genus, Family, Order, Class, Phylum and Kingdom.

To give you an idea of how this works, this is how the **lion** is classified:

Kingdom	**Animalia**	This group includes all the animals. Another kingdom would be Plantae or plants.
Phylum	**Chordata**	This group includes all the vertebrates or animals with a backbone.
Class	**Mammalia**	This group includes all mammals.
Order	**Carnivora**	This group includes all carnivores.
Family	**Felidae**	This group includes all cats.
Genus	***Panthera***	This group includes all big cats that can roar. These are the tiger, lion, jaguar and leopard.
Species	***Panthera leo***	This is the lion.

The more specific the classification, the more similar the animals are to others in the group. For example, the mammals grouped in the **family** Felidae are more similar to one another than the mammals grouped in the **order** Carnivora. And these are more similar than the mammals grouped in the **class** Mammalia.

This system of classification is used all over the world! It's a way to identify and share the information about all the plants and animals found on earth.

Habitats are home

Mammals choose to live in different habitats, such as grassland, woodland, forest or sea. While some mammals can only live in one or two kinds of habitats, other mammals can live in many different kinds of habitats. Here are two examples:

Oribi
Ourebia ourebi
(H: 60 cm; 14 kg)

A specialist

Oribis need a very special kind of habitat. They are called habitat specialists. They prefer to live in short, moist grassland that gives them the particular types of short-grass plants they like to eat. They also need patches of tall grass for cover to hide from predators. Oribis are now threatened in many areas because so much of their habitat has been taken over by farms and towns.

A generalist

Common duikers can live in many different kinds of habitats, as long as there is some cover to hide from predators. They eat the seeds, leaves, stems and flowers of a wide variety of plants. They are called habitat generalists. Habitat generalists usually survive better than habitat specialists because they are more adaptable. This is because they are able to survive in many different environments.

Jelger Herder

Common duikers eat a variety of plant food, such as leaves, fruits, seeds, flowers, grass and roots.

Look at the map on the opposite page to learn more about the different kinds of habitats in southern Africa.

A **habitat** is defined by its particular kind of climate (weather), geology (type of rocks found there), topography (the surface features of an area) and group of plants and animals.

Habitats in southern Africa

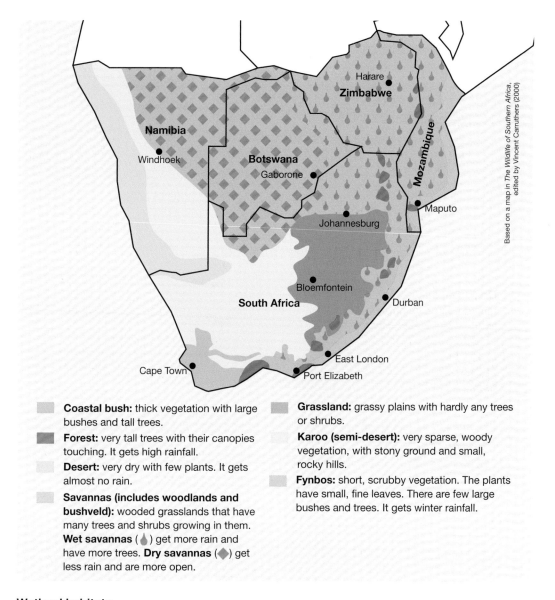

Based on a map in *The Wildlife of Southern Africa*, edited by Vincent Carruthers (2000)

Coastal bush: thick vegetation with large bushes and tall trees.

Forest: very tall trees with their canopies touching. It gets high rainfall.

Desert: very dry with few plants. It gets almost no rain.

Savannas (includes woodlands and bushveld): wooded grasslands that have many trees and shrubs growing in them. **Wet savannas ( )** get more rain and have more trees. **Dry savannas ( )** get less rain and are more open.

Grassland: grassy plains with hardly any trees or shrubs.

Karoo (semi-desert): very sparse, woody vegetation, with stony ground and small, rocky hills.

Fynbos: short, scrubby vegetation. The plants have small, fine leaves. There are few large bushes and trees. It gets winter rainfall.

Wetland habitats

Wetlands are places with water, from small streams and ponds to large rivers and lakes. They are habitats found within all the other habitats listed on this page. We have not included the sea or estuaries in this book.

Mammal diets

Carnivores

Carnivores are animals that eat other animals. Examples are **lions**, leopards, cheetahs and wild dogs. They are skilled stalkers and killers.

Well-adapted for hunting, they have excellent eyesight and hearing, sharp teeth and bodies designed for speed or power.

Jelger Herder

Carnivores need binocular vision to catch or hunt prey. Read how this helps on page 15.

Each carnivore has its own way of finding and catching food. Getting enough food is crucial to its survival. Have a look at the hunting behaviour of some large carnivores on pages 27–35.

Omnivores

Omnivores are animals that eat plants and animals. African civets and jackals mainly eat animals but they also add plant food to their diets. Read about them on pages 33 and 40.

Others, like warthogs, monkeys and baboons, mainly eat plant food but add animals to their diets. Read about them on pages 59–60.

Rudi Jeggle

Black-backed jackals are omnivores.

Aardwolves, pangolins, aardvarks and some bats only eat other animals, like carnivores do. But we can call them **insectivores** because their diet only consists of insects.

Herbivores

Herbivores are animals that only eat plants. But they don't all have the same diet. There are browsers, grazers and mixed feeders. Have a look below.

By having different diets there is less competition between herbivores and more food to go around. We can often guess what a herbivore eats by looking at the habitat it prefers to live in.

Grass grazers

Some herbivores mostly graze grass and are called grazers, like buffalo, **white rhinos**, zebras and wildebeest.

White rhinos prefer living in grassland or open savanna habitat.

Bush browsers

Some herbivores mostly browse on shrubs and trees and are called browsers, like black rhinos, giraffe, kudu, nyala and **bushbuck**.

Bushbuck prefer living in dense bush and forest habitat.

Mixed feeders

Some herbivores, like **elephants** and impala, browse and graze, depending on what is best to eat at the time. In the wet season they will eat mainly green grass, but in the dry season they will switch to eating bushes and trees.

Elephants live in a variety of habitats, from grassland to forest to desert.

Other ways to spread the load

Herbivores also eat different parts of the plant. For example, giraffes eat in the tops of trees, kudu in the middle and duikers at the bottom. Grazers do a similar thing. Some eat tall grass and others eat short grass. This means that there is more food to go around.

Amazing adaptations

To survive, an animal must be able to adapt. Adaptation is how an animal's body or behaviour changes so that it can survive better in its environment.

Coats of camouflage

Most predators use camouflage to hide from prey. This increases their chances of catching something to eat. Some have a coat colour that is the same as the environment they live in. For example, **lions** are the colour of dry grass. Others, like **leopards**, have spots. The base coat is the same colour as the habitat, but the spots break up the outline of the body so that the animal blends in with the background. A leopard can become almost invisible at night (see also page 16 about camouflage).

Jelger Herder

Lion

Carl Haycock

Leopard

Eyes that can see in the dark

A game drive at night is an exciting time to spot nocturnal predators. Their eyes shine brightly in the spotlight. This is because there is a special layer of cells at the back of each eye, which acts like a mirror shining the light back at you. Large eyes and pupils let in as much light as possible. The special layer and large pupils give nocturnal animals the ability to see in the dark.

Alan Calenborne

A **bushbaby's** large eyes shine in the dark.

Finding food

Animals have to eat to survive. Animals have many amazing adaptations to help them find food. Here are just a few examples.

A trunk for everything

An **elephant**'s trunk is very powerful but also incredibly flexible. It has about 40 000 muscles and two finger-like tips at the end. The trunk is not just used for feeding but also holding, touching, smelling, drinking, dust-bathing, communicating with other elephants, and even snorkelling while bathing. An elephant has an acute sense of smell and can find underground water by smelling the earth above.

An elephant's trunk is an incredibly useful tool.

Binocular vision

When an animal has both eyes sitting right at the front of its head, it has what is called binocular vision, which means that both eyes work together. Binocular vision allows an animal to judge distance accurately. Predators need binocular vision for hunting. They can tell how far away the prey is from them. Antelope have their eyes on the sides of their head. They are able to look out for predators from many directions.

Samango monkeys move around in trees by leaping from branch to branch. They need binocular vision or they might end up on the ground!

Long legs, long necks

Giraffe have exceptionally long necks. Like humans and most other mammals, they have seven bones in their necks. But a giraffe's neck bones are much larger and longer! This allows them to reach up into the tops of trees, where other herbivores cannot reach. Their legs are also especially long. When they walk, first both legs on one side of the animal's body move together, then the legs on the other side move together. This way, the legs don't get tangled up.

The isiZulu name for a giraffe is *indlulamithi*, which means 'taller than the trees'. Their height gives them an excellent view for spotting predators.

Escaping predators

Another very important part of survival is being able to escape predators. Have a look at some of the ways mammals do this.

Camouflage

Most animals have coats that give them camouflage to hide from predators. The coat colour of a **springbok** is the same colour as its environment. The outline of its body is also broken up by a dark line. It has dark upper parts and a pale belly and chest. This helps it blend in with its environment.

Other herbivores have stripes or spots for camouflage. See pages 47 and 48.

Springbok live in dry, open country.

Group living

Animals living in a group have a much better chance of surviving because members work together to escape predators.

Zebras live on open grassy plains in large groups. Many animals together have a better chance of spotting predators. Their best defence is to spot the predator before it spots them. If they are threatened, they bunch together and stampede in a large group. The black and white stripes of the zebras blend into one another. This confuses predators because it becomes difficult to pick one animal out of the herd.

The stripes of zebras blend into one another.

Many mammals only see in black and white, so they rely more on shape and movement to see one another. This is why camouflage works so well.

Body armour

Another way to survive a predator's attack is by having body armour.

Sharp quills

A **porcupine** has sharp spines, called quills, for protection. To protect itself, it stamps its feet and rattles its quills. It makes the quills on its back stand up so it looks bigger. It will run backwards at the enemy to try to stab it. It will also hide down a burrow, leaving only its quills sticking out.

Porcupine
Hystrix africaeaustralis
(L: 75–100 cm; 10–24 kg)

Dangerous horns

Many antelope, such as **gemsbok**, use their horns to defend themselves against predators. They might back themselves into a bush so that they cannot be attacked from behind. Many antelope have dangerously razor-sharp horns.

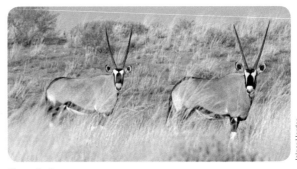

Jelger Herder

Gemsbok

Tough scales

A **pangolin** is covered in a layer of tough, heavy scales. To protect itself, it rolls into a ball with its head and legs tucked safely under its heavily armoured tail. The scale edges are sharp and can leave serious cuts.

David Bygott

Pangolin

Pangolins are considered to be symbols of good fortune in certain parts of Africa. To see one is said to guarantee you a good day, and to find a pangolin scale could give you a charmed life.

Space to live

What is a home range?

When an animal finds a space to live in a habitat, we call it the animal's **home range**. A home range provides the animal with all the things it needs to survive, such as food, water and shelter.

Female cheetahs have a home range

Female **cheetahs** live alone or with their cubs. They find a space that gives them enough food to eat and a place to rest and hide their cubs, safe from other predators. Female cheetahs living in the same area will share the habitat.

Cheetah
Acinonyx jubatus
(H: 60–80 cm;
40–80 kg)
Prefers open areas like open savanna with grassland.

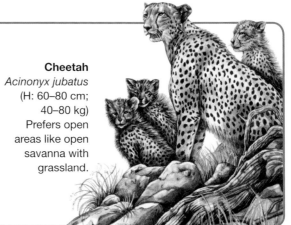

What is a territory?

When an animal starts defending a space in the habitat, that space is called a territory. The owner of the territory will fight to protect it. It is protecting something that is not in great supply, like a special feeding ground or a mate.

Female ground squirrels keep a territory

Female **ground squirrels** live together in family groups with their young. They dig a large burrow, called a warren, for themselves. The warren is an incredibly important place, where they sleep, find shade, escape predators and raise their young.

Female ground squirrels defend a territory around the warren. They will chase off their squirrel neighbours and even fight with them to protect the warren.

Jelger Herder

Scent signals

Animals communicate with one another by leaving scent signals in the habitat. The scent signals are made by scent-marking objects in the environment using special scent glands. They also urinate and defecate to leave information about themselves. The urine and faeces carry the scent of the animal.

Scent signals give important information on whether an animal is male or female, whether it is the owner of the territory or not, and whether or not it is ready to mate. Read about the other ways animals communicate on pages 20–21.

Klipspringer signals

Male and female **klipspringers** have a large scent gland in front of each eye for marking their territories. By pushing the tip of a twig into the eye gland, they leave a black, sticky fluid with their scent on the twig. They also mark their territories with large piles of dung. These can be up to three metres wide and ten centimetres deep.

scent gland

Alan Calenborne

Klipspringers live in rocky habitats. They have the amazing ability to jump and climb rocks.

Impala signals

Adult male **impala** only set up territories in the breeding season. During this time they fight with each other by clashing and pushing with their horns. The winner marks his territory with large piles of dung. He also rubs the scent gland on his forehead on bushes in his territory. This leaves an oily fluid carrying his strong-smelling scent. These scent signals tell other male and female impala that he is the owner of the territory and is ready to mate.

Carnivores mark their territories with piles of dung, called latrines. Herbivores also mark their territories in the same way, but the dung piles are called middens.

Animal communication

Animals have developed many different ways to communicate with one another. This is very important in the social lives of animals. Animals communicate using sound, sight, touch and scent. Read about scent signals on page 19.

Using sound

Vervet monkeys have at least 36 different calls that they use to express themselves! Every vervet can recognise the call of the other vervets in its own and neighbouring troops.

Vervets also use different alarm calls for different predators. For other animals it can be a lot simpler. For example, rabbits thump their feet and porcupines rattle their quills as alarm signals.

Sally van der Woude

Like vervet monkeys, **baboons** have over 30 different calls to communicate different things to one another.

Elephants can communicate with one another over many kilometres using infrasound. These are sounds so low that human ears cannot hear them. The sound is a rumbling or deep growling believed to come from the stomach. The sound is felt through the elephant's sensitive feet and trunk. This solves the mystery of how elephants are able to find one another across miles of savanna!

Using sight

Animals use coat colours and patterns as signals. Many have obvious marks on their behinds or tails. These marks help to keep the group together when moving through long grass or escaping predators. For example, the tails of many antelope are fluffy and have white hair underneath. As they dash through the bush their tails lift up and the white, fluffy part flashes. It signals to others in the group that 'danger is close' or 'follow me'.

Alan Calenborne

The white tip of a **leopard**'s tail helps her cubs to follow her in long grass.

Other ways of using sight

Animals have many different ways of expressing themselves using their faces and body postures. Cats, like **cheetahs** and leopards, use a variety of signals. Vervet monkeys have at least 60 different body signals! These signals help animals to understand one another and avoid fighting.

This kind of expression on a cheetah's face means that it is getting ready to defend itself. Its ears are back, its eyes are narrowed and its mouth is half open.

Using touch

Animals living in family groups use touch as a way of bonding with one another and keeping things friendly in the group. Elephants often touch or stroke each other when they are resting or drinking. Mothers often stroke their young. Lions greet each other by rubbing their heads and then their sides together. **Zebras** groom one another by nibbling at each other's necks and backs.

Jelger Herder

Zebras may stand in pairs with their heads resting on each other. This is a way of bonding. They can also help to keep the flies off each other's faces and look out for predators in all directions.

Finding a mate

While survival is tough, finding a mate is tougher! Usually it's the males that have to fight for the females. This is risky business because males may be seriously injured or even die in a fight.

'This is my territory!'

An adult male **white rhino** sets up a territory where there is a good supply of food and some shade for resting. He also knows this area will attract female rhinos, and because he owns the territory, he will be the first to mate with them.

When another male rhino intrudes into his territory, he will confront the intruder. To signal that he is the territory owner, the rhino keeps his head raised and ears cocked. If the intruder drops his head and puts his ears back, it means he will give way and accept that the other rhino is dominant. But if the intruder does not back off, they will fight.

Two male white rhino confront each other.

Stronger as a group

Male **cheetahs** often get together in a group. They are stronger as a group and are better at defending a territory against other male cheetahs. The males usually place their territories where the female cheetahs live. This means they stand a better chance of finding a mate. Not all male cheetahs get a chance to own a territory. Some wander thousands of kilometres or die before they ever get a chance to own a territory or find a mate.

Male cheetahs mark their territories by spraying urine at special marking places around their territory. This tells other male cheetahs to keep out.

Jelger Herder

Some animals don't keep a territory

Elephants, buffalo, zebras and wild dogs are examples of animals that don't keep territories. But they still have to find a mate and the males will fight for the females if they have to.

When an animal is called the **dominant** animal, it's because this animal has proved that he or she is the strongest and fittest in the group or area. He or she is often the older, more experienced animal.

Zebras fight

A dominant male **zebra**, called a stallion, keeps a group of females, called a harem. He has to protect the group from other males. If another male tries to take over the group, they will fight. They try to bite each other, wrestle each other to the ground and sometimes kick. Kicking can be serious if a leg or jaw is broken.

Plains zebras will fight for a mate.

Elephants stand tall

Male **elephants** find out who is dominant by sizing each other up. They meet face to face, holding their heads high, trunks hanging down and ears spread. The male that can hold his head higher than the other is the dominant animal. He gets to mate with the females first. Elephants avoid fighting unless they really have to, like when a female is present and ready to mate.

Male elephants size each other up.

Conservation matters

Conservation is a way of looking after and taking responsibility for the natural world. Conservation came about because many animals and plants were disappearing from the Earth.

The main problem

Mammals have lost much of their habitat to humans. Humans have turned the indigenous habitat where mammals once lived into towns, farms and exotic forests. Many large mammals, such as elephants, lions and buffalo, now only survive well in nature reserves and parks. Conservationists are trying to increase the size of nature reserves or to join nature reserves together to make larger reserves.

Struggling to survive

Wild dogs normally wander over huge areas. But because of human development, like farms and towns, wild dogs can't do this anymore. They have lost so much of their habitat to humans that they are struggling to survive. It's hard to keep them inside small reserves or to find reserves big enough to conserve them. They clash with human activities outside reserves and pick up diseases that can kill them.

Jelger Herder

Africa's most threatened carnivore – learn more about wild dogs on page 32.

Places too small to live

In the past, large mammals, like **elephants**, were able to roam over enormous areas, without fences! Now they are mostly stuck inside small, fenced reserves. Their numbers grow inside these small places and they can end up damaging or destroying the habitat because they can't move to other areas to find food.

Jelger Herder

Elephants naturally break down trees for food. This has benefits for many animals. Read why on page 43. However, in small reserves they can destroy the habitat.

Other problems

Many animals suffer at the hands of humans. They are poached, hunted or poisoned, nearly to extinction, like the Cape mountain zebra (see page 48). Black and white rhinos have always been threatened by poaching, and today conservationists fear they will soon be extinct.

Black and white rhino horn is so valuable that today it is worth more than gold. The horn is illegally shipped to the Far East where it is carved to make special dagger handles or crushed into powder for Chinese medicine. Rhino horn is not actually made of bone but a substance known as keratin, which is exactly what human hair and nails are made of.

White rhino

Rudi Jeggle

What can you do to help?

- Save the habitat and the environment by using resources, such as food, water, paper and electricity, with care! If these precious resources are wasted, more farms are needed to produce more food, more exotic forests are needed to make more wood and paper, more land is needed to supply more electricity, and more wetland habitat is lost to get more water.
- Grow your own food in a vegetable garden.
- Recycle all your waste, such as paper, tins, plastic and glass.
- We have listed some websites at the end of this book where you can learn how to save electricity.
- We have also listed some websites where you can learn more about conservation efforts to save the animals and how you can help.

An endangered rabbit

The **riverine rabbit** is endangered. This means it may go extinct soon if we don't look after it. It is only found in the karoo habitat. Find where this habitat is on the habitat map on page 11. The riverine rabbit prefers habitats along rivers, where there is good soil to make burrows that don't collapse. But the riverine habitat has been destroyed by farming and the rabbits have been hunted by dogs.

Riverine rabbit

Barbra Werneyer

▶ The mammals

Cats

The cat family includes the largest cats, such as lions and leopards, and the smallest, such as servals and African wild cats. They are all carnivores. While most cats are solitary, which means they live alone, lions are social, which means they live with others of the same kind.

Lions are the only truly social cat

Female **lions** and their young live in a group called a pride. There are many benefits to living in a group, such as having help with hunting and looking after the cubs. The pride always has a dominant male or a group of male lions called a coalition. The male lions defend the pride's territory and mate with the females. Male lions form coalitions because they are stronger as a group. The mane of male lions is used to protect the neck from the sharp claws of other males when they fight over territories.

Lion *Panthera leo*
(H: 1 m; male: 180–230 kg; female: 113–160 kg)
Lives in most habitats, except forest.

Living alone

Other cats like **leopards**, caracals, servals and African wild cats live alone, except when the mother is looking after her cubs. Males and females only come together long enough to court and mate. A benefit of living alone is that you don't have to share your food with anyone else!

Leopard *Panthera pardus* (H: 70–80 cm; 40–70 kg)
Lives in wide variety of habitats, not desert.

Female cheetahs live alone while male cheetahs live alone or in groups. Read more about this on pages 18 and 22.

How do lions hunt?

Lions hunt by stalking and chasing. Female lions do most of the hunting. They hunt together, which improves their hunting success. They stalk low and carefully. The chase usually begins from about 20 to 30 metres away. They rush at the herd, surprising the animals and causing panic. Some of the lions try to cut off a fleeing animal. One lion leaps onto the rump or shoulders and throws it off balance. As soon as it falls, it is grabbed by the throat and strangled or suffocated.

Food choices

Lions feed on large prey, like **zebra**, wildebeest, giraffe and buffalo. They can bring down animals twice their own weight. This is because lions are large and powerful and hunt in groups. They hunt mostly at night, because their night vision is six to eight times better than that of their prey.

Lions reach a maximum speed of 60 kilometres per hour. They can only keep this up for about 100 metres. Compare this with cheetahs on page 29. This is why lions rely on stalking while cheetahs rely on speed to catch fast-moving antelope.

'But Grandma, what big teeth you have!'

Carnivores like lions and leopards have four long, pointed canine teeth, called eyeteeth, used for holding their prey and ripping or tearing the meat. They are also used as weapons. They have blade-like cheek teeth, which are used for slicing through the meat.

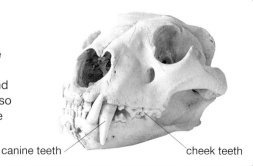

canine teeth   cheek teeth

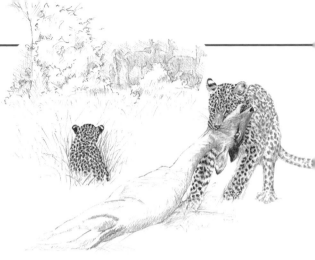

How do leopards hunt?

Leopards hunt by stalking and pouncing. They mostly ambush their prey. They don't do much chasing. They lie in wait in long grass or up trees. When the prey is very close, they pounce. They will often wait in areas where they know prey will pass by, like well-used paths to waterholes. The prey is strangled and dragged to a hiding place.

Food choices

Leopards hunt mainly at night and have a wide choice of food. They prefer impala, springbok, reedbuck and the youngsters of larger prey, such as hartebeest, wildebeest and zebras. They also eat birds, rabbits, hares, monkeys, baboons, reptiles and even invertebrates.

If its prey is large, like an impala, a leopard will wedge it tightly into the fork of a tree to protect it from competitors, like lions and hyenas. Then it will feed on the animal over two or three nights.

Spot the difference

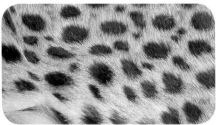

The leopard's coat is made up of three to six spots grouped in a circle on the sides and back of the body – read on page 14 about camouflage.

The cheetah has single black spots that get closer together on the legs, underside, neck and upper head.

How do cheetahs hunt?

Cheetahs hunt with speed. They are designed for speed, with sleek bodies, long legs and light builds. They stalk their prey when there is cover, like shrubs or long grass. Their long tails act as rudders to help with balance while chasing after the prey. The chase can begin from 70 to 300 metres away from the prey. They can run up to 112 kilometres per hour, averaging about 64 kilometres per hour. These are the speeds that cars move on the roads! Cheetahs are the fastest land mammals.

A cheetah knocks its prey over by striking it on the backside or tripping it up. The prey is strangled and then dragged to cover before the cheetah starts feeding. Once a cheetah leaves its kill, it never returns because other predators might come to feed on the leftovers. Unlike lions and leopards, cheetahs hunt in the day, hardly ever at night. This helps them avoid these large predators, which often steal their prey or try to kill them.

Food choices

Cheetahs prefer medium-sized buck, such as impala, gazelles, springbok and reedbuck. But they also take any youngsters or weaker animals because they are easier to catch.

Cheetahs are the only cats without retractable claws. This means that the claws don't pull back inside the foot when they are not being used. These claws give cheetahs better grip on the ground when they are running at top speed.

A small cat specialist

Servals are experts at catching rodents and birds that live in tall grass. They have large ears and acute hearing for pinpointing exactly where prey is hiding, even underground. They have long legs, which make them the tallest of Africa's small cats, so they can stand higher in the grassland. This improves their ability to hear and see prey.

Serval *Leptalurus serval* (H: 50 cm; 8–13 kg)
Prefers well-watered grasslands, reed beds or edges of forest near water.

How do they hunt?

Servals use their long legs to make high leaps as they pounce on their prey. The leaps can be one to four metres long and up to one metre high. They come down on prey with both front feet. They are so quick and agile they pluck birds out of the air with a high jump and a bat with their paw. They will also dig for prey and hook them out with their claws.

Conservation matters

Servals are not considered threatened but they have been affected by habitat loss and are now extinct in the Western Cape. Farmers also kill them because they think servals kill their sheep and poultry, but it's usually caracal or black-backed jackal (see opposite and page 33). Servals were hunted a great deal at one stage for their beautiful fur, but this is now illegal.

A true wild cat or not?

African wild cats can live just about anywhere but they are threatened because they breed with our pet cats. There are hardly any pure African wild cats left in places where humans live. They are only really protected in places far away from people.

How do they hunt?

African wild cats hunt by stalking and pouncing. They hunt alone and at night. They creep as close as they can without being seen, and then after a short run and a few pounces, the prey is caught. They eat rats, mice, rabbits, hares, small birds like starlings, doves, reptiles, frogs and invertebrates.

African wild cat *Felis lybica*
(H: 35 cm; 4–5 kg)
Lives in most habitats,
except forest and desert.

A cat with long, black ear tufts

A **caracal**'s coat is coloured for camouflage. But its face and ears stand out! The ears are black on the outside, white on the inside and have tufts of long black hair on the tips. When two caracals meet they communicate by expressing themselves with their faces. The long tufts on their ears move and flick as the face or ears move. One of the ways animals communicate with one another is by using signals that other animals can see. Read about the other ways animals communicate on pages 20–21.

Caracals live alone and are active at night. When they hunt their ears fold back so they are better camouflaged.

Caracal *Felis caracal*
(H: 40 cm; 7–19 kg)
Lives in most habitats,
but not thick forest.

Wild dogs

Team-work

Wild dogs live in large packs of about 10 to 15 animals, sometimes up to 40 animals. They work together as a team. They hunt in packs and help to feed and look after the mother and cubs. They have patchy and blotchy coats for camouflage. This breaks up the body so the shape and movement of the dogs, especially in a pack, becomes confusing to prey.

Wild dog *Lycaon pictus*
(H: 68 cm; 24–30 kg)
Lives in desert areas and open savanna.

How do they hunt?

A pack of wild dogs walks through their habitat looking for prey. Once prey is found, one dog starts the chase. The rest of the pack spreads over a wide area. The dogs chase their prey over long distances until it's exhausted.

Wild dogs have long legs and slim bodies, which gives them speed and endurance. They can run up to 60 kilometres per hour for up to five kilometres. They take it in turns to chase the prey. Then they surround it and disembowel it while it is still standing. Although this seems cruel, it is no more cruel than the way other predators kill their prey.

Food choices

Wild dogs eat buck such as impala, springbok and reedbuck. They also take the youngsters of buck and smaller animals like hares. They often take weak and unhealthy animals first and so help to keep the prey populations fit and healthy.

The wild dog is one the most endangered mammals in Africa. Read more about this on page 24.

Jackals

Jackals mate for life

Male and female jackals mate for life. The pair keeps a territory, which they both scent-mark and defend against other pairs. They use burrows dug by other animals, like porcupines and aardvarks (see page 61), to raise their litters. Sometimes brothers and sisters help the parents raise the pups by bringing them food and looking after them while the parents are away hunting.

Myles Veysey

Black-backed jackals stay together for life, unless one of them dies.

Successful hunters

Black-backed jackals mostly hunt for their food. They eat young antelope, rabbits, rats, mice, reptiles, birds, carrion and invertebrates. They hunt larger prey in pairs and will take old, weak or sick animals first. They also eat fruit and seeds, which means jackals are omnivores. They search for prey with their excellent hearing and smell. They pounce when they see an opportunity to get a meal.

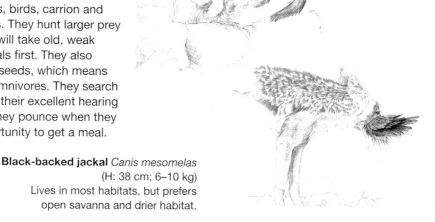

Black-backed jackal *Canis mesomelas*
(H: 38 cm; 6–10 kg)
Lives in most habitats, but prefers
open savanna and drier habitat.

Skilful scavengers

Jackals are also scavengers. They follow other predators, like lions, to get leftovers at a carcass. But they can also smell a dead body from over a kilometre away! They look out for vultures soaring over carcasses and then compete with them for the leftovers.

Hyenas

Sloping bodies

Hyenas have sloping backs because their front legs are longer and larger than their back legs.

They are also loaded with muscles in their shoulders and necks.

Jelger Herder

Spotted hyena *Crocuta crocuta* (H: 70–80 cm; 65–70 kg)
Prefers open to closed savanna.

Powerfully built

The front part of henas' bodies are so powerfully built that they can pull whole pieces, like a leg, off a carcass and carry it high off the ground. **Brown hyenas** also carry heavy loads of food back to their dens, often over long distances. Hyenas have large skulls with powerful jaws and teeth that can splinter and crush bones, and cut through animal hide.

Spotted hyena

Why have longer hair?

The brown hyena has much longer hair than the **spotted hyena**. The long hair keeps the brown hyena warm in its desert-like habitat when it gets very cold at night. When threatened, it lifts up the hair to make itself look bigger and more scary. It forages on its own, so it doesn't have group protection like a spotted hyena does, which forages in groups.

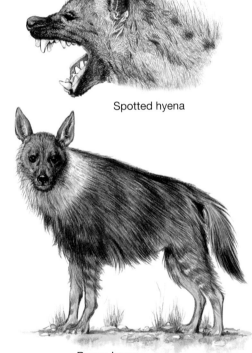

Brown hyena *Hyaena brunnea* (H: 80 cm; 45 kg).
Prefers desert, karoo and dry savanna.

Brown hyena

Have a look at the habitat choices of the hyenas. Then look at the habitat map on page 7 to see where these animals are found in southern Africa.

Superb scavengers

Hyenas have excellent hearing. They listen for the dying calls of prey when they have been caught by other predators or the fighting among other predators at their kills. They have an acute sense of smell. This allows them to sniff out dead carcasses from kilometres away. They also follow lions and finish off the carcass once they have left the kill.

Skilled hunters

Spotted hyenas are skilled hunters. More than half their food comes from hunting. They often choose the easiest animals to catch, like young, sick or old ones. They are mostly active at night. When hunting, they run at a group of animals to scatter them. Then they run after a chosen animal until it is too exhausted to escape. They pull it down and rip open the soft area of the stomach. The prey dies within a few minutes.

Bush cleaners

Hyenas clean up the veld of rotting carcasses and prevent the spread of disease. Their stomachs can actually dissolve bone and even teeth, so their dung is rich in calcium. Many animals, like tortoises, eat hyenas' dung to get calcium for making their shells hard and producing eggs.

A hyena's dung is very white because it contains so much calcium from the bones it eats.

Fierce competition

There is fierce competition between carnivores for food. They often steal one another's kills. This is called kleptoparasitism. Lions are the strongest, followed by spotted hyenas, wild dogs, brown hyenas, leopards, and then cheetahs.

Cheetahs are the weakest because they are designed for speed and not for strength. They often have their kills stolen by other carnivores. They either eat their kill quickly or hide it before eating it.

Leopards, although powerful predators, live on their own and have their kills stolen by predators that live in groups, like lions and spotted hyenas. Leopards often drag their prey up a tree to stop it from being stolen.

Group size counts!

The size of the animal often determines who will be the winner. The lion is by far the largest and heaviest predator in Africa. But the size of the group also affects the outcome of a battle.

- Although wild dogs weigh the least, they are often in large packs and can chase off larger, heavier carnivores, like leopards.
- Lions can be outnumbered by a group of spotted hyenas and chased off. Hyenas have powerful, bone-crushing jaws, which can cause serious injuries to lions. See page 34.

Cheetah

Leopard

Cheetahs and wild dogs avoid bumping into lions and spotted hyenas by hunting during the day, when the bigger predators are usually resting or asleep.

Aardwolves

A termite-eater

Aardwolves mainly eat harvester termites. These termites have an underground nest but they come to the surface in their thousands to collect and eat dry grass. Aardwolves use their large tongue to lick them up.

Aardwolves find the termites mostly by listening for them. Their large ears move around constantly and independently as they search for the noises of termite activity.

Aardwolf *Proteles cristatus*
(H: 50 cm; 8.5 kg)
Lives in a wide
variety of habitats,
not forest.

Why an earth-wolf?

'Aardwolf' is Afrikaans for 'earth-wolf' because these animals live in holes in the ground and look a bit like wolves. They dig their own burrows, or they use old porcupine or aardvark burrows. See these animals on pages 17 and 61. Aardwolves have a number of burrows in their territory. They use them for shelter, escaping predators, sleeping or as dens for their cubs.

Harmless helpers

Aardwolves are killed by farmers who think they kill their livestock. But they don't have the teeth for it! Their cheek teeth are like small pegs so they could never chew up the meat.

Aardwolves can eat up to 250 000 termites a night, so they help to keep termite numbers down. Termites can have a huge impact on grazing land because they remove tonnes of grass ever year.

Polecats and badgers

Hidden defences

Striped polecats and **honey badgers** have bold coats of black and white, which are a warning to other predators. The warning is that they have hidden defences that they will use if they are not left alone!

Striped polecats first growl and scream to scare away predators. They raise the hair on the body and tail so they look twice as big as usual. Their best line of defence is that they can produce a disgusting-smelling fluid from the scent gland under their tails that lasts for hours.

Striped polecat *Ictonyx striatus*
(L: 62 cm; 713–970 g)
Lives in most habitats.

Honey badgers are so fearless that only lions, leopards and clans of spotted hyenas really threaten adult badgers. They have even been known to chase off lions! They have powerful gripping jaws, crushing teeth, sharp claws and thick skin, which they can turn around in when held and bite back. They can also produce a disgusting smell from the scent gland under their tails.

Honey badger (ratel) *Mellivora capensis*
(L: 95 cm; 12 kg)
Lives in most habitats.

What do they hunt?

Polecats and honey badgers hunt mostly at night. They use their long, strong claws to dig prey out of the ground. Polecats mostly eat insects and mice, while honey badgers eat a wide variety of food, including dangerous scorpions and snakes, bee larvae, honey and fruit.

Honey badgers are killed by honeybee and poultry farmers because they raid beehives and poultry houses. Conservationists are trying to educate farmers to get them to use friendlier methods of stopping badgers.

Otters

Life in water

Otters spend a great deal of time in water. They have long, thick, muscular tails used to push them through the water. They have stiff whiskers used for sensing prey under murky water. Their coats are made up of dense fur, called guard hair, covering a fine, tightly packed underfur. This helps to repel water so they don't become heavy and sink. It also dries quickly.

Spot the difference

The **spotted-necked otter** has webbed and clawed feet and a streamlined body. It is an excellent swimmer. It hardly ever moves away from water. It finds prey in the water, mostly by sight, catching it in its mouth. It prefers fish, but will also eat crabs, frogs and invertebrates. The very strong teeth crush the shells and bones of the prey.

The **African clawless otter**'s hands are not webbed or clawed. The hands are used for feeling for prey, such as crabs, in murky water or under rocks and in sand. It catches and holds prey with its fingers. The skin is rough under the fingers for holding onto slippery prey. It eats crabs, frogs and fish, but also insects, reptiles and even birds. It spends more time in shallow water and on land than the spotted-necked otter. It also lives by the sea.

Spotted-necked otter *Lutra maculicollis*
(L: 1 m, 3–5 kg)
Lives in large rivers, lakes, dams and swamps with plenty of water.

whiskers

African clawless otter *Aonyx capensis*
(L: 1.5 m; 10–18 kg)
Lives in rivers, lakes, dams, marshes, small streams, estuaries and sea.

Otter dung

Otters are seldom seen but their dung, filled with crab shells and fish scales, often gives them away. They make large dung piles, called latrines, to mark the area where they live. Read on page 19 how these become scent signals for other otters.

Civets and genets

Confusing animals

Civets and genets are usually spotted at night on their own. It can be confusing to tell them apart. **African civets** are far larger than genets, with a much shorter tail. The long tail of genets helps them to keep their balance when climbing trees. Civets have a black mask across their eyes. The colours and patterns on their coats help to camouflage them at night.

Spot the difference

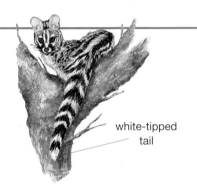

white-tipped tail

African civet *Civettictis civetta*
(L: 1.2–1.4 m; 11–12 kg)
Lives in woodland, forest and wet savannas where there is plenty of water.

Small-spotted genet *Genetta genetta*
(L: 80–95 cm; 1.8–1.9 kg)
Lives in many different kinds of habitats, but prefers drier areas.

Finding food

Civets and genets both hunt for food mostly on the ground. But genets are better climbers and climb to hunt or escape predators. During the day, civets and genets shelter in trees, under bushes or in holes in the ground, where they are hidden from predators. They are omnivores, and eat insects, fruit, reptiles, birds, frogs, small mammals, green grass and nectar.

Millipede rings are found in genet and civet dung. These mammals eat toxic species that are often avoided by other predators.

black-tipped tail

There is another genet called the **large-spotted genet**. It has a black-tipped tail unlike the small-spotted genet, which has a white-tipped tail. Large-spotted genets are sometimes spotted in the suburbs at night so look out for them and take care not to frighten them. They hunt in trees or on the ground and nest in holes or even roofs of houses.

Large-spotted genet
Genetta tigrina (L: 100 cm)

Mongooses

About mongooses

There are at least ten different mongooses in southern Africa. Different species live in different habitats. Some live alone or in pairs, while others live in large family groups. Knowing these differences helps us to identify them!

Living together

Yellow mongooses and **suricates** are very sociable mongooses. They both live in family groups. They live in very open habitat so predators are able to spot them easily. Often these two species will live together and share the same warren. They help one another with digging the burrows, watching out for predators and giving alarm calls to warn one another of danger. A mongoose's main enemies are birds of prey, honey badgers and jackals.

Although yellow mongooses live in family groups at the warren, they always look for food on their own.

Suricates are well known for standing up straight on their back feet. They do this to look out for danger.

the black-tipped tail is a good way to identify it

Living alone

The **slender mongoose** lives on its own. It prefers habitats with thick vegetation, including bushveld, forest and riverine habitats. This habitat provides them with good cover to escape from predators.

Slender mongoose *Galerella sanguinea*
(L: 60 cm; 460–640 g)
Lives in a wide variety of habitats,
not deserts.

Very sociable mongooses

Dwarf and **banded mongooses** are very sociable. They live in close family groups of up to 30 animals. They can do this because there is enough food in the habitat to supply the whole group. Living in a group helps tremendously with watching out for predators.

Dwarf mongooses need many termite mounds in their habitat for sleeping in at night, escaping predators and as dens for their young. All members in the group have duties to do. Some guard the group, others babysit and others attack predators or intruders.

Dwarf mongoose
Helogale parvula
(L: 38 cm; 260 g)
Prefers open savanna.

What do they eat?

Mongooses are omnivores. They mainly eat invertebrates, like beetles, grasshoppers and termites, but also lizards, snakes, rodents, birds, fruit and plants.

Banded mongoose
Mungos mungo (L: 60 cm; 1.4 kg)
Lives in dense savanna and some forests.

Continuous chatter

Banded and dwarf mongooses spread out when they go looking for food. But they 'talk' to one another all the time to keep in touch. Each mongoose in the group has its own particular voice. If there is danger, one of them warns the group and they will dive for cover. They know where all the hiding places are in the area, like holes in the ground, fallen trees or termite mounds.

Banded mongooses looking for food.

Elephants

The biggest land animal

The **African elephant** is the biggest living land animal. An adult elephant needs to eat about 200 kilograms of food a day to keep its huge body happy. It also needs to drink about 80 litres of water a day. Elephants switch their diet to get the best nutrition all year round. In the rainy season they eat fresh green grass but in the dry season they eat leaves, branches and the bark of trees and bushes.

Elephants use their big ears for cooling themselves down. Their ears are packed with blood vessels, so when they flap their ears, air flows over them and cools the blood.

African elephant *Loxodonta africana*
(male H: 3.2–4 m, W: 5 000–6 300 kg;
female H: 2.5–3.4 m, 2 800–3 800 kg)
Lives in most habitats.

Scientists use an elephant's ears and tusks to identify individual elephants. Next time you are watching a herd, see if you can notice any differences between the elephants.

They benefit others

Elephants naturally break trees and bushes for food. By doing this, they benefit plants and other animals.

- They open up and create paths in the bush that animals prefer to use.
- They clear bush, which allows more grass to grow in the habitat. This helps grazers, such as wildebeest and zebra.
- They also bring food within reach of browsers when they break down the branches of trees.

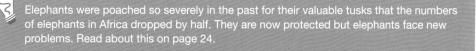

Elephants were poached so severely in the past for their valuable tusks that the numbers of elephants in Africa dropped by half. They are now protected but elephants face new problems. Read about this on page 24.

Rhinos

Powerful but threatened

Black and **white rhinos** are enormous and powerful animals. Have a look at how much they weigh! But they have very small eyes and poor eyesight. This makes them easy to poach and they nearly disappeared at one stage because people hunted them for their horn. Read about this in the section on conservation matters on pages 24 and 25. Both black and white rhino are protected species.

Scent signals

Male rhinos are very territorial animals. They communicate using their dung. They create large dung piles, called middens, to tell other male rhinos, 'This is my territory, keep out!'. The male rhino uses his back feet to spread his dung. His feet get coated in the scent. As he walks he leaves a scent trail around his territory. Read on page 22 how owning a territory gives a male rhino a better chance of finding a mate.

Spot the difference

hooked lip

square lip

Black rhinoceros *Diceros bicornis*
(H: 1.6–2 m; 800–1 100 kg)
The black rhino has a hooked lip, which can curl around branches or grasp leaves, shoots and twigs. It is a browser and prefers to live in dense bush or thickets.

White rhinoceros
Ceratotherium simum
(H: 1.8m; 1 600–2 300kg)
The white rhino has a square lip, which acts like a lawnmower. It is used for grazing short grass. It prefers to live in open grassy savannas.

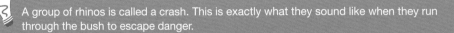

A group of rhinos is called a crash. This is exactly what they sound like when they run through the bush to escape danger.

Hippos

Half in and half out the water

Hippos spend half their lives in water. They have their eyes, ears and nose at the top of their heads so they can submerge themselves under the water but are still able to hear, see and breathe. They have a layer of thick fat under the skin to keep them warm in cool water. They also have special glands in the skin that produce a sticky, bright-red fluid to stop sunburn. At night and often on overcast days they come out to graze on grass.

Hippos have completely bare skin. This makes them very sensitive to the sun's rays. They stay in the water most of the day.

'This is my territory!'

Hippos live in groups of about 15, with females, their young and a dominant bull. A bull shows his dominance by yawning to display his formidable teeth. If male hippos fight over a territory, they slash at each other with their teeth. The teeth can be up to 50 centimetres long. A dominant bull marks his territory by wagging his tail as he defecates. This spreads his dung.

Hippopotamus *Hippopotamus amphibius*
(H: 1.5 m; 1 500 kg)
Lives where there is water to wallow
in and short grass to graze.

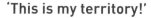

Hippo help

- Hippos create well-worn pathways from the rivers to their grazing grounds. This benefits other animals that prefer to use paths through the bush.
- In certain areas, hippos keep the grass short, which benefits other grazers that prefer short grass.
- They transfer nutrients from the grassland, where they eat, to the river, where they wallow. The nutrients released from their dung feed many fish and invertebrates.
- They keep the waterways open by their movements and open up new channels in the wetland.

Hippos prefer to graze near the safety of the water but will wander several kilometres to find food.

Buffalo

Social living

Buffalo are very social mammals. They live in large herds of up to 1 000 animals, made up of smaller family groups. Large herds like these can trample down and open up tall grassland. This helps other herbivores because it makes it easier for them to spot predators. It also benefits other grazers because they can get into the grassland more easily to find food.

Adult male buffalo have thick, heavy bosses. The boss is the area in the middle of the head where the horns join together. Males use them for fighting over who is dominant in the group.

boss

Buffalo *Syncerus caffer*
(H: 1.6 m; 750 kg)
Prefers open woodland or
savanna with plenty of grass.

Escaping danger

Buffalo raise their noses into the air to smell for danger. They also use their sense of smell to sniff out the best patches of grass. Buffalo stick together in a group and stampede. This makes it difficult for predators to pick out and attack individuals. Only lions can really prey on buffalo because of their large size, but in a large herd it's difficult to bring one down.

Friendly relationships

Oxpeckers find their food on herbivores, such as buffalo, giraffe, zebras, antelope and warthogs. The birds help these animals by removing the ticks and bloodsucking flies from their skin with quick, scissor-like movements of their bills. The birds also let them know if danger is about.

These heartwater ticks carry disease.

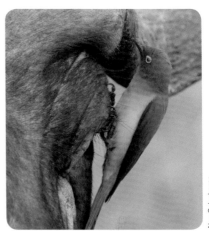

Alan Calenborne

A buffalo lets an oxpecker remove ticks from places it can't reach.

Giraffe

The tallest animal in the world

The **giraffe** is the tallest animal in the
world. It finds food right up high in the tree
canopies, where most other animals cannot
reach. It has a long, curling, thick and
leathery tongue, which can stretch out about
45 centimetres to wrap around twigs and
leaves. A very flexible upper lip is protected
by short, dense hairs and the roof of its
mouth is tough and horny. It picks leaves,
shoots, flowers, seed pods and fruit off trees
and bushes.

Giraffe defend themselves against predators
by kicking with their front and back feet.
This can kill a lion.

Giraffe *Giraffa camelopardarlis*
(male H: 4.9–5.2 m, 990–1 400 kg;
female H: 4.3–4.6 m, 700–970 kg)
Prefers to live in dry savannas.

Bone-eaters

Many animals, such as giraffe, warthogs
and porcupines, suck on or eat bones to get
calcium and phosphate. This is like taking
your vitamins!

This giraffe is chewing on a bone.

Jelger Herder

*Next time you are in the game reserve, have a look at a giraffe's horns. Adult female and
young giraffe have thin horns with tufts of hair. Adult male giraffe have larger horns without
hair. As male giraffe age they grow other bony, horn-like bumps on their heads. The males
use their heads like big clubs when they fight for dominance and a chance to mate.*

Zebras

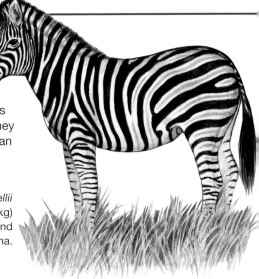

Tough survivors

Zebras can survive under poor conditions. This is because they can eat very poor quality grass. They can do this because they have a large gut that can process lots of food at a fast rate. Out of all this food they get enough nutrition to survive.

Plains (Burchell's) zebra *Equus burchellii*
(H: 1.3 m; 300–320 kg)
Lives in open woodland
and grassland savanna.

Lessons on relationships

Zebras and wildebeest are both grazers, so they will mix together in nutrient-rich areas where there is ample food. They both benefit because it means there are more eyes watching out for danger. There is little competition between the two grazers because zebras prefer tall grass to eat and wildebeest prefer short grass.

Read on page 16 how zebras use camouflage to escape predators. Also have a look on page 23 to see how male zebras often have to fight for mates.

Conservation matters

Cape mountain zebras nearly went extinct in the early 1900s because they were overhunted. There were fewer than 100 animals left until conservationists came to the rescue. They established a reserve, called the Cape Mountain Zebra National Park, to protect them. Their numbers are increasing but they are still a conservation concern. These zebras are only found in mountainous grassland habitat in South Africa's south-western Cape.

Cape mountain zebra
Equus zebra zebra
(H: 1.3 m; 245 kg)

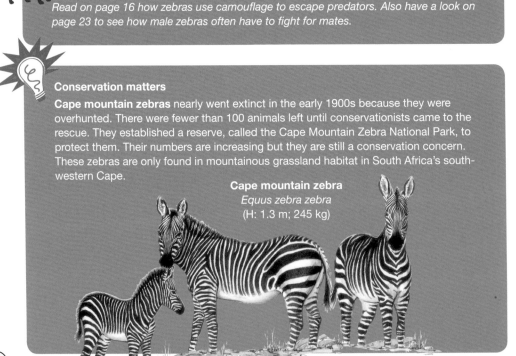

Antelope

Horns and hooves

All antelope have horns, although in some species only the males have them. Antelope horns have a bony core coated with a hard material made mostly of keratin. Keratin is a protein that hair, nails and skin are made of. Antelope also all have hooves. Their hooves are split down the middle, which divides the hoof into two 'toes'. All antelope are herbivores.

Jelger Herder

Spiraled-horned antelope

Kudu, eland, nyala and bushbuck are all browsers and have spiral-shaped horns. They eat fruit, seeds, pods, flowers, leaves and bark from bushes and trees. They are very picky feeders and only select the best-quality material. They use their lips, not their tongues, to gather food. Read about kudu, nyala and bushbuck on page 50.

A kudu's horns are used by males to fight for a mate and to fight off predators. They are also used to break down higher branches of trees to get to the leaves.

The largest antelope in southern Africa

Eland need to eat plenty of food to keep their huge bodies happy. When they are not eating, they are chewing the cud to get more nutrition out of the food. They don't need water to survive. Read below what 'chewing the cud' means.

Eland *Taurotragus oryx*
(H: 1.6 m; male: 700 kg, female 450 kg)
Lives across a wide variety of habitats,
not desert or thick forest.

'Chewing the cud'

Some herbivores, like buffalo, giraffe, eland and many other antelope, 'chew the cud'. Cud is regurgitated larger, tougher parts of plants that need to be chewed again so the stomach can get the most nutrition out of them too.

Escaping predators

The three antelope on this page can be confusing to tell apart! They live mostly in small groups in bushy or wooded areas. Their coat colour is broken by stripes or spots, which helps them to blend in with the background. This is excellent camouflage in the patchy sunlight of woodlands and forests. They usually freeze and then scatter when they are threatened.

Spot the difference

Kudu *Tragelaphus strepsiceros*
(male H: 1.4 m, 230 kg; female H: 1.2 m, 155 kg)

- **Kudu** prefer woodland or dense savannas and hilly terrain.
- Kudu males have long, spiraled horns.
- They are usually spotted in small groups.
- Their coats are reddish in colour.

Nyala *Tragelaphus angasii*
(male H: 1.1 m, 110–125 kg;
female H: 1 m, 55–75 kg)

- **Nyala** prefer bush or thickets along or close to rivers.
- Nyala horns twist and are shorter than kudu horns.
- They are usually spotted in small groups.
- Their coats are greyish in colour.

Bushbuck *Tragelaphus scriptus*
(H: 70–80 cm; male 30–60 kg;
female: 24–35 kg)

- **Bushbuck** prefer dense woodland and bush near rivers, and often forests.
- They are shy and secretive.
- They have white spots on their sides.
- They are smaller than nyala and kudu.
- They are usually spotted alone.

Have a look at the different habitats found in southern Africa on the map on page 11. Can you find the habitats on the map where the antelope shown above would live?

The horse antelope

Sable antelope and **gemsbok** are called the horse antelope because they are shaped like horses. They have handsome coats and formidable horns. The striking black coat patterns help with communicating to one another over long distances in their open habitat.

Spot the difference

Sable antelope prefer grassland in dry, open woodland. Their mouths are long and narrow so they can eat tufted, medium-to-tall grass. Sable need to drink water every day.

Sable antelope *Hippotragus niger* (H: 1.35 m; 230 kg)

Gemsbok live in dry, open areas, like semi-desert to desert habitats. They don't need water to survive. They meet their water requirements by eating water-storing plants, like wild melons and cucumbers.

Gemsbok *Oryx gazelle* (H: 1.2 m; male 240 kg; female: 210 kg)

Have you ever noticed that the coat of young animals is often very different to that of their parents? This is because they are often hidden away in the veld until they are old enough to join the group. The young sable above would camouflage well in long dry grass.

How do gemsbok survive without drinking?

- They graze at night when the temperature has dropped and plants absorb moisture from the air.
- They can let their body temperature rise to 45°C. This would kill other animals! This means they don't have to sweat to keep cool and lose water from their bodies.
- They produce concentrated urine, which means there is very little water in it.

The 'beasts'

Wildebeest and **hartebeest** have sloping backs. This is because the front parts of their bodies are well developed and higher than the back parts. This added strength allows them to canter for long periods without getting tired. This helps particularly when they migrate. Wildebeest and hartebeest will migrate incredibly long distances to find better feeding grounds with fresh grass.

Spot the difference

Blue wildebeest *Connochaetes taurinus*
(male H: 1.5 m, 250 kg;
female H: 1.3 m, 180 kg)
Prefers open savanna grassland.

Red hartebeest *Alcelaphus buselaphus*
(H: 1.25 m; 120–150 kg)
Prefers dry, open savanna.

Social lives

Wildebeest live in family groups of 20 to 30 animals. But adult male wildebeest are often spotted alone. This is because they keep a territory, which they protect by chasing away other males or fighting with them using their horns. A male wildebeest with a territory chases female herds into his territory so he can mate with them.

Carl Haycock

The red hartebeest is one of the fastest antelope in southern Africa. It outruns most predators.

If a male wildebeest has shade or water in his territory, the female wildebeest will stay in his territory for longer.

Water-loving antelope

Waterbuck and **reedbuck** prefer to live near water. They also need cover, like tall grass or bushes, to hide from danger. Waterbuck will sometimes run into deep water to escape being caught.

male

Waterbuck *Kobus ellipsiprymnus* (H: 1.3 m; male: 260 kg; female: 230 kg; horns: 75 cm). Lives in savannas and woodlands close to water.

A signal for dominance

Male waterbuck and reedbuck use their horns to fight to see who is the strongest and fittest. The winner is called the dominant male. One of the signals for dominance in male waterbuck and reedbuck is to stand tall and 'proud'. Other males keep their heads low unless they want to challenge the dominant male.

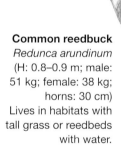

male

Common reedbuck *Redunca arundinum* (H: 0.8–0.9 m; male: 51 kg; female: 38 kg; horns: 30 cm) Lives in habitats with tall grass or reedbeds with water.

Flashy warning signs

If reedbuck suspect danger is nearby, they give short whistles as alarm calls to others in the group. As they gallop away snorting, they flash the white hair underneath their bushy tails. This is a signal that says to other reedbuck, 'danger is close-by, follow me'.

Toilet-seats on their behinds

Waterbuck are identified by the toilet-seat-shape on their behinds! This is thought to be a clear signal for others to follow when there is danger close-by. It also helps young ones not to get lost in the long grass.

Alan Calenborne

Female waterbuck

Unlucky impala

Impala live in small to large groups and are one of the most common antelope seen. Because they live in groups, are common and medium-sized, impala are favourite prey of large carnivores like lions, hyenas and cheetahs. So how do they escape being eaten?

Jelger Herder

Impala *Aepyceros melampus* (male H: 90 cm, 65 kg; female H: 85 cm, 45 kg)
Prefers open savanna woodland.

Blending in

Impala coats blend in with the habitat. They have dark upper parts and pale bellies and chests. This breaks up the outline of the body, so when they freeze if there is danger close-by, they are hard to spot. They also bunch together so that they blend in with one another. There are also many eyes in the herd looking out for danger.

Living in bushy country

Impala prefer open, grassy areas in fairly bushy country. They can spot a predator more easily in the open grass but, when threatened, they scatter into the surrounding bush.

Giant leaps

When alarmed, impala blow or snort to warn one another of danger. When running, they scatter in all directions. They confuse predators with enormous leaps of up to three metres high and 11 metres long.

Read on page 19 how male impala set up territories in the breeding season to find a mate.

Diving duikers

Duikers prefer to live in habitats that give them cover for hiding from predators. 'Duiker' is an Afrikaans name that means 'diving'. They are named 'duikers' because of their habit of diving for cover when danger is near. Eagles, pythons and baboons prey on them. Duikers are browsers. They eat shoots, fruit and berries.

Scent signals

All duikers have a narrow slit on either side of the nose. These are special scent glands that produce a sticky or oily substance carrying the duikers' smell. Duikers live alone or in pairs. To keep the bond between pairs, they press their scent glands together. Males and females keep a territory, which they mark by rubbing their scent glands against tree branches and other objects. Males also press their glands together before a fight.

Spot the difference

scent gland

Common duiker *Sylvicapra grimmia*
(H: 50 cm; 18–21 kg)
Lives in a wide variety of habitats.

Red duiker *Cephalophus natalensis*
(H: 42 cm; 12 kg)
Prefers forests and dense woodland with water.

scent gland

Blue duiker *Philantomba monticola*
(H: 35 cm; 4.5 kg)
Prefers forest and dense bush with water. This is the smallest antelope in southern Africa.

Dwarf antelope

Dwarf antelope are small antelope that all defend territories. They live on their own, in pairs or in groups with their young. They have large, round scent glands in front of each eye, which they use for marking vegetation around their territory. Have a look at the klipspringers on page 19. The pair or group also uses the same dung piles, called middens, to mark the territory and keep them together.

Large ears in the open

Steenbok live on their own or in pairs in open habitats. They have big, round ears, which they use to listen out for predators. Large ears are like sound traps, which carry the sound down into the ear drums. Steenbok lie down low in long grass to hide but will dash away suddenly at high speed when discovered. They are experts at making sudden, quick turns to escape predators.

Steenbok *Raphicerus campestris* (H: 50 cm; 11 kg)
Lives in open grassland or open savanna.

Hidden under cover

Suni prefer habitats where the trees grow so closely together that they are called closed habitats. These habitats give them plenty of cover for hiding from predators. They are very small and shy and not often seen. They are the second-smallest antelope in southern Africa. Suni have lost a great deal of their habitat to farming. They are also caught by dogs and snares. They are very rare in South Africa and are protected.

Suni *Neotragus moschatus* (H: 36 cm; 5 kg)
Lives in dry thickets, closed woodland and forest.

Oribis are also part of this group. Have a look on page 10.

Hyraxes

Rock-loving dassies

Dassies, or rock hyraxes, are very sociable animals. They live in groups of up to 35 animals on rocky outcrops or cliffs. They are very agile and can bound up and down steep rocks very easily. They can do this because they have thick, rubbery pads under their feet. The pads have sweat glands that become sticky with sweat. This gives them excellent grip.

Rock hyrax (dassie) *Procavia capensis* (L: 50 cm; 3.5 kg)
Lives on rocky outcrops and cliffs in grassland, savanna, woodland and forest.

Escaping predators

Dassies can't dig. Instead, they use rock crevices in their habitat for shelter and protection from predators. They have many long, sensitive whiskers on their faces for feeling around in these dark places. There is always one dassie on look-out while the others are feeding to warn the group of any danger.

Dassies are prey to many animals, including eagles, owls, leopards, caracals and snakes. Their eyes have a special sun-shield layer so they can look straight into the sun, as eagles often attack with the sun behind them.

Dassies have two small, sharp front teeth that continue to grow their whole lives. They are called tusks because they are designed just like elephant tusks, only far smaller. They are used for protection, and males use them when fighting for territories.

Primates

Monkeys, baboons and bushbabies are all primates. For their body size, they have large brains compared to most other mammals. Their bodies are very agile and they have prehensile hands and feet. These adaptations make them excellent climbers of trees with very rich social lives.

This baboon primate is very skilful with its hands and feet.

Are all primates social?

Monkeys and baboons are very sociable. They eat, sleep and rest together in groups. They also warn and protect one another from predators, like leopards and eagles. Bushbabies forage on their own at night, when they are protected by the dark. They sleep together in groups of two to eight in the day, hidden in leafy nests or holes.

Bushbabies

Bushbabies have large eyes for seeing at night. They have large ears and acute hearing. They listen out for approaching insects and then snatch them out of the air with their hands. But they mainly eat the fruit and gum from Acacia trees.

Bushbabies have strong muscular back legs for leaping across tree branches. They can leap up to ten metres! Their long, bushy tails help them balance as they jump. Bushbabies keep in touch with one another in the dark with their loud crying and noisy screaming. They sound like crying babies.

Lesser bushbaby *Galago moholi*
(L: 30–40 cm; 150 g)
Lives in wet and dry forest and open woodland.

Everybody knows their place

Monkeys and baboons live in troops of 15 or more. Troops are made up of many families living together. To keep order in the troop, there is a hierarchy in place. In a hierarchy, each member either dominates or is dominated by another member. Everybody gets to know their place in the hierarchy right from birth. Animals higher up in the hierarchy get the best food, first chance to drink and best places to rest.

Spot the difference

Vervet monkey *Cercopithecus aethiops* (L: 1 m; 5 kg)
Vervet monkeys live mainly in trees in a variety of wooded habitats.
They need trees for food and safety from predators.

Chacma baboon *Papio ursinus* (L: 1.35 m; male: 30 kg, female: 16 kg)
Baboons stay mainly on the ground.
They live in a variety of open habitats. They prefer areas with mountains, hills and forests that have tall trees or rocky cliffs for shelter and protection.

What do they eat?

Baboons and monkeys are omnivores. They eat plant material like fruit, flowers, leaves and seeds but also invertebrates, mice and rats, reptiles, ground birds, eggs and hares.

Why do animals groom each other?

Grooming is a very important part of the social lives of many animals. When they groom, they pick off bits of dead skin, ticks and other parasites. Grooming is also a very important way of bonding group members together and keeping things friendly.

Pigs

Pigs have a large head with a long, muscular snout and an excellent sense of smell. Their noses are used to dig in the earth in search of food. This is called rooting. The end of the nose is round and flat, like a fleshy disk, and has a good sense of touch. The nostrils can close so the pigs don't breathe in soil and dust while they are rooting around. They eat grass, grass roots, bulbs, tubers, invertebrates, frogs and carrion.

Spot the difference

Warthog *Phacochoerus aethiopicus*
(H: 70 cm; 60–100 kg)

- **Warthogs** are mainly active during the day.
- They prefer open habitat like grassland and savanna.
- They are covered in a thin layer of hair.
- They use burrows for shelter and protection, and as dens to hide their young.

Bushpig *Potamochoerus porcus*
(H: 60–85 cm; 60 kg)

- **Bushpigs** are mainly active at night.
- They prefer habitats with cover, like forests, dense bush and tall grassland.
- They are covered in a thick layer of long hair.
- They build nests out of grass and leaf litter. They also find shelter in dense thickets.

Why have a mud bath?
Warthogs, elephants, buffalo and rhinos have thick, leathery skin with very little hair. They like to take mud or dust baths. This protects their skin from sunburn, helps to keep them cool and gets rid of ticks and other parasites, which can carry disease.

These warthogs are taking a mud bath.

Aardvarks and pangolins

These unusual mammals are insectivores. They only eat ants and termites. They use a very long, sticky tongue to lick up their prey. They are active mostly at night and sleep in burrows during the day.

Earth-pigs that dig

The **aardvark** is a powerful digger. Its back and front feet are armed with large, powerful claws, for digging open ant and termite nests.

It has a long pig-like snout and an acute sense of smell. It keeps its snout close to the ground while searching for the underground nests of its prey. Its eyesight is poor so it uses its long, tube-like ears and excellent hearing to listen out for predators at night.

Aardvark *Orycteropus afer*
(L: 1.4–1.8 m; 40–70 kg)
Lives in a wide variety of habitats,
avoids desert and forest.

Armoured ant-eaters

Pangolins are covered in a layer of thick, heavy scales. Read on page 17 how they use their body armour as protection against predators. Their back legs are powerfully built to carry the heavily armoured body.

They find their prey with an acute sense of smell. They use their large front claws to scratch open ant nests. They can also produce a stinking fluid from the scent gland under their tail to scare off predators.

Pangolin *Manis temminckii*
(L: 1.1 m; 7–10 kg)
Lives in a wide variety of habitats,
from forest to open savanna.

Many animals rely on the burrows dug by aardvarks. The burrows can be 6 metres deep. Porcupines, warthogs, hyenas, lizards, snakes, pangolins and many other animals use the burrows for shelter, escaping predators, and as dens for their young.

Shrews and elephant-shrews

Shrews and **elephant-shrews** are often mistaken for rats or mice (see page 65), but they are actually not in the same group. They are both meat- or insect-eaters. They both have long snouts, which they use, along with an excellent sense of smell, to sniff out prey.

Small-eyed shrews

Shrews have a wedge-shaped snout and very small eyes with poor eyesight. Their tiny bodies burn up energy so rapidly that they need to eat every few hours to stay alive. They eat invertebrates, lizards and frogs.

Shrews dig burrows for shelter, hiding their young, escaping predators and storing food. They have scent glands along the sides of their bodies. They rub the glands onto the walls of their burrows as a way of communicating with others. The musky smell from the scent glands will put off many predators, but not owls.

Forest shrew *Myosorex varius* (L: 12 cm; 15 g)
Lives in moist, dense vegetation in a wide variety of habitats. The mother shows her young around the area where they live. Each one holds onto the other with its teeth. This is called caravanning. This way they don't get lost.

Elephant-shrews

Elephant-shrews have a long, trunk-like snout and large eyes. The snout moves around constantly as it sniffs the air for prey. They mostly eat ants and other insects.

Elephant-shrews' back legs are much longer than their front legs. They use their long back legs to escape predators by leaping and bounding across the ground. They also have large ears for listening out for predators. They drum their back feet on the ground to let predators know they have been spotted.

Four-toed elephant-shrew *Petrodromus tetradactylus* (L: 35 cm; 160–200 g)
Lives in forests with dense undergrowth.

Rabbits and hares

Rabbits and hares live on plant food, like grasses, leaves, bark and roots. Their front and cheek teeth grow throughout their lives. This is necessary because they feed on the very tough parts of plants, which wears their teeth down. They have a second stomach-like bag in their gut that breaks down the food further so the nutrition is not wasted. They also eat their own faeces to get more nutrition out of it.

Escaping predators

Rabbits and hares have long back legs, used for running and bounding. They have large eyes on the sides of their head so they can see what's coming from many directions. They have large ears, which they use to listen out for predators. Birds of prey, caracals, jackals and many other predators prey on them.

Spot the difference

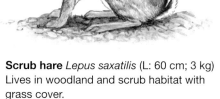

Smith's red rock rabbit *Pronolagus rupestris* (L: 45 cm; 1.5 kg)
Lives in rocky habitats with grass cover.

- Most rabbits live in burrows called warrens. **Red rock rabbits** do not dig burrows but use rock crevices or dense vegetation.
- The young rabbits are born in the warren in a warm nest lined with hair and soft grass.
- Rabbits are born blind, without any hair, and helpless. Their eyes don't open for many days.
- Rabbits use cover to escape predators and protect the young.

Scrub hare *Lepus saxatilis* (L: 60 cm; 3 kg)
Lives in woodland and scrub habitat with grass cover.

- Hares use shallow hollows pressed into the soil by the body and hidden in grasses or bushes as nests.
- They are born covered with warm fur and with open eyes. They can run soon after birth.
- Hares freeze to protect themselves and then dash off, zig-zagging through the grass. They can reach speeds of 70 kilometres per hour.

Learn about the riverine rabbit on page 25. It is the most endangered mammal in southern Africa.

Rodents

Mammals with large, chisel-shaped front teeth are part of the rodent family. Rodents continually gnaw at things to keep their teeth the correct length. If not worn away, the teeth would grow nearly 10 centimetres a year.

Molerats

Common molerats dig or chisel away at the soil using their enormous front teeth. They are adapted to life underground and are shaped like cylinders to fit neatly into the tunnels they dig. Their eyes and ears are tiny because they don't need to see or hear underground.

They use touch and smell to find food and to communicate with one another. They live on roots, bulbs and tubers that plants have underground as food-storage organs.

Common molerat
Cryptomys hottentotus
(L: 15 cm; 125 g)
Lives in a wide variety of soils, but not clay soil.

Squirrels

Squirrels live in small family groups, but forage on their own for fruit, seeds, shoots, roots and insects. They always stay close to holes in the ground or in trees where they can hide to escape danger. Read about ground squirrels on page 18.

Tree squirrels are incredible climbers. They run up and down tree trunks and leap metres across branches. Their bushy tails help them with balance when landing and acts as a rudder when leaping. The tail is also used for warmth, by wrapping it around their bodies, and for communication, by bobbing it up and down.

Tree squirrel
Paraxerus cepapi
(L: 34 cm; 190 g)
Lives in woodland habitat, but not forest.

Mice and rats

There are 57 species of mice and rats in southern Africa. This is the second biggest group of mammals after bats (there are about 74 species of bats). The main difference between rats and mice is that rats are usually larger. They eat seeds, green plant food and insects. Mice and rats live in many different types of habitat.

Spot the difference

Striped mouse *Rhabdomys pumilio*
(L: 20 cm; 45 g)
Striped mice live in grassy areas in a wide variety of habitats. They dig long burrows under bushes or build round nests in clumps of grass.

Vlei rat *Otomys irroratus*
(L: 24 cm; 120 g)
Vlei rats live in marshy areas or damp grasslands. They build round nests on dry, raised ground or in clumps of grass.

Food for many

Mice and rats are a very important source of food for many predators, including leopards, jackals, genets, servals, mongooses, reptiles and birds of prey. They escape predators by dashing for cover and hiding in burrows or crevices that are too small for predators to enter. They also run, leap, climb or swim if they have to.

Mice and rats have coats the colours of their environment. This helps to camouflage them from predators. They have very long, sensitive whiskers for finding their way around inside their burrows or holes, where it's dark.

Jelger Herder

Grey climbing mouse

The porcupine is southern Africa's largest rodent. Read how it defends itself against predators on page 17.

Bats

Flying mammals

Bats are the only mammals that can truly fly. They flap their wings like birds. A bat's wings are made up of a thin layer of skin that stretches across four long bony fingers and are joined to long arms and short back legs.

Insect-eating bats

Insect-eating bats have tiny eyes and poor eyesight. They find their prey and way around at night using ultrasound. Ultrasound is sound waves too high-pitched for human ears to hear.

Egyptian free-tailed bat
Tadarida aegyptiaca
(L: 11 cm; 15 g)
Lives in a wide
variety of habitats.

Echolocation

Insect-eating bats produce high-pitched squeaks and then listen for the sound bouncing back from an insect or another object. This is called **echolocation**. They start hunting by using about five pulses of ultrasound a second as they fly around. When they find an insect, this will increase to about 200 pulses a second to help it zoom in on its prey. Insect-eating bats have large ears that stick straight up so they can pick up sound coming back to them.

Cape serotine bat
Eptesicus capensis
(L: 8.5 cm, wingspan:
24 cm; 6.5 kg)
Lives in a wide variety
of habitats.

There are over 70 bat species in southern Africa. Ten species are threatened with extinction. The biggest danger to bats is the destruction and disturbance of their habitat and homes. People killed them in huge numbers in the past and still do.

Roosting in the day

Bats sleep during the day in caves, old buildings and trees. This is called roosting. They have five clawed toes on their back legs. These are used for hanging upside down in the roost. They have a clawed thumb that sticks out at the front that is used for moving around the roost. They hunt for food when the sun goes down.

Fruit-eating bats

Fruit-eating bats, like **Wahlberg's epauletted fruit bat**, are larger bats with bigger eyes and smaller ears than insect-eating bats. They use their eyesight and sense of smell to find food. They eat fruit but also flowers and nectar.

Wahlberg's epauletted fruit bat *Epomophorus wahlbergi* (L: 14 cm; 100 g) Lives in forest and riverine woodland. It roosts with other bats in trees during the day.

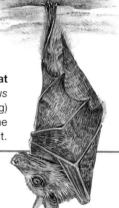

clawed thumb

Egyptian fruit bats form colonies of many thousands. They roost in caves and old mine-shafts. They are the only species of fruit bat that uses echolocation. Read what echolocation is on the opposite page. Echolocation helps these bats to find their way in darker places.

Egyptian fruit bat *Rousettus aegyptiacus* (L: 15 cm; 130 g) Lives in forest, savanna or riverine woodland with plenty of ripe fruit.

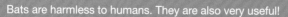

Bats are harmless to humans. They are also very useful!

- **Fruit-eating bats** pollinate the flowers of the plants they visit. They also spread the seeds from the fruit they eat.
- **Insect-eating bats** eat harmful insects, such as mosquitoes, and crop pests, like locusts. One insect-eating bat can eat up to 10 times its weight in insects every night!

Birds

▶ All about birds

Learning about birds

There are over 900 bird species living in southern Africa. That's a lot of bird species to learn if you are interested in learning them all! And there is a lot more to understand about their behaviour. Although there are so many birds, there are actually a lot of similarities between them. For example, certain birds have exactly the same shaped body, beak and feet. These birds are put into the same bird group. For example, bee-eaters are one bird group made up of nine different species.

In this section, we will introduce you to some of these fascinating bird groups. Then we look at a few of the birds within a bird group to see some of their extraordinary differences. For example, the colour of their feet and feathers or the places they live might be different. We also look at many of the amazing adaptations and habits these birds have developed in order to survive.

The one thing that birds have that no other animal group in the world has is feathers! We talk more about the amazing adaptations of feathers on pages 76–77.

White-fronted bee-eaters belong to the bee-eater group. Read more about them on page 107.

Alan Calenborne

The value of birds

Birds are a link in the food chain

A food chain is how all living things depend on each other as food to survive. For example, birds eat a variety of plants and animals. Birds, in turn, are eaten by other animals. The example below shows a very simple food chain. Without the bird as a link, this food chain would break down.

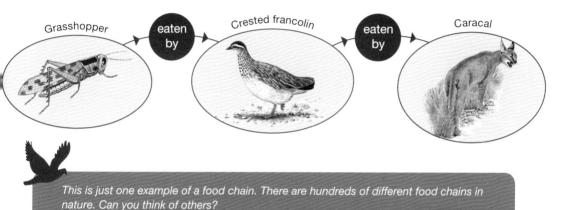

Grasshopper — eaten by — Crested francolin — eaten by — Caracal

This is just one example of a food chain. There are hundreds of different food chains in nature. Can you think of others?

Birds help others

Birds help plants by dispersing their seeds and pollinating their flowers. Birds also help humans by feeding on insect pests, such as ticks, flies, mosquitoes and locusts, and keeping their numbers down. These pests can harm us or the things around us that we depend on.

A **lilac-breasted roller** feeds on a locust. Locusts can become pests to farmers by eating their crops.

A **Cape sugarbird** drinks the nectar of Protea flowers and, in doing so, pollinates them.

The science in a name

Every bird is given its own Latin (or scientific) name and common (or English) name. The Latin name is used all over the world. It is written in italics. Italic letters slope to the right, *like this.* The common name can vary from country to country. Look at the example below.

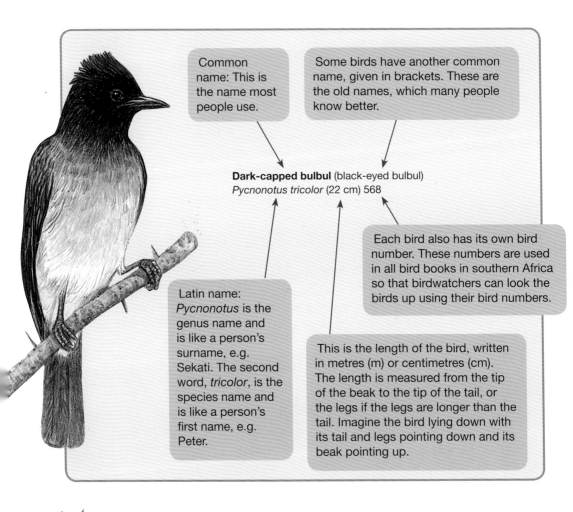

Common name: This is the name most people use.

Some birds have another common name, given in brackets. These are the old names, which many people know better.

Dark-capped bulbul (black-eyed bulbul)
Pycnonotus tricolor (22 cm) 568

Each bird also has its own bird number. These numbers are used in all bird books in southern Africa so that birdwatchers can look the birds up using their bird numbers.

Latin name: *Pycnonotus* is the genus name and is like a person's surname, e.g. Sekati. The second word, *tricolor*, is the species name and is like a person's first name, e.g. Peter.

This is the length of the bird, written in metres (m) or centimetres (cm). The length is measured from the tip of the beak to the tip of the tail, or the legs if the legs are longer than the tail. Imagine the bird lying down with its tail and legs pointing down and its beak pointing up.

Ornithology is the study of birds. A scientist who studies birds is called an ornithologist.

Classification helps identification

When we classify a bird, we put it into groups with other animals or birds that have the same or similar features. **This helps us identify or find out what it is.** Birds in the same group are similar – they are like one another. Birds in different groups are different – they are unlike one another. Examples of group names are Genus, Family, Order, Class, Phylum and Kingdom.

To give you an idea of how this works, this is how the **dark-capped bulbul** is classified:

Kingdom	**Animalia**	This group includes all the animals. Another kingdom would be Plantae or plants.
Phylum	**Chordata**	This group includes all the vertebrates or animals with a backbone.
Class	**Aves**	This group includes all birds.
Order	**Passeriformes**	This group includes all the passerines. See what this means on page 94.
Family	**Pycnonotidae**	This group includes bulbuls, brownbuls and greenbuls.
Genus	***Pycnonotus***	This group includes all the bulbuls.
Species	***Pycnonotus tricolor***	This is the dark-capped bulbul.

The more specific the classification, the more similar the birds are to others in the group. For example, the birds grouped in the **family** Pycnonotidae are more similar to one another than the birds grouped in the **order** Passeriformes. And these are more similar than the birds grouped in the **class** Aves.

This system of classification is used all over the world! It's a way to identify and share the information about all the plants and animals found on earth.

Habitats are home

Different birds, different habitats

Birds choose to live in different kinds of habitats, such as grasslands, forests or woodlands. A habitat must provide them with all the things they need to survive, such as food, water and shelter. Some birds can only live in one kind of habitat. For example, saddle-billed storks need large wetlands to survive. They are called habitat specialists.

Other birds, such as crows and sparrows, can live in many different kinds of habitats. They are called habitat generalists. Habitat generalists usually survive better than habitat specialists because they are more adaptable.

Look at the map on the opposite page to learn more about different habitats in southern Africa. Here's a good tip: It's easier to identify a bird if we know what habitat it prefers.

Alan Calenborne

The **saddle-billed stork** lives next to large rivers, lakes and wetlands. It is a habitat specialist. This stork is endangered because it is losing its wetland habitat to humans.

White storks live in grasslands, farmers' fields and open woodland, and sometimes around wetlands. They are habitat generalists.

There are two different storks on this page. Can you spot their differences? Read more about storks on page 119.

A habitat is defined by its particular kind of climate (weather), geology (type of rocks found there), topography (the surface features of an area) and group of plants and animals.

Habitats in southern Africa

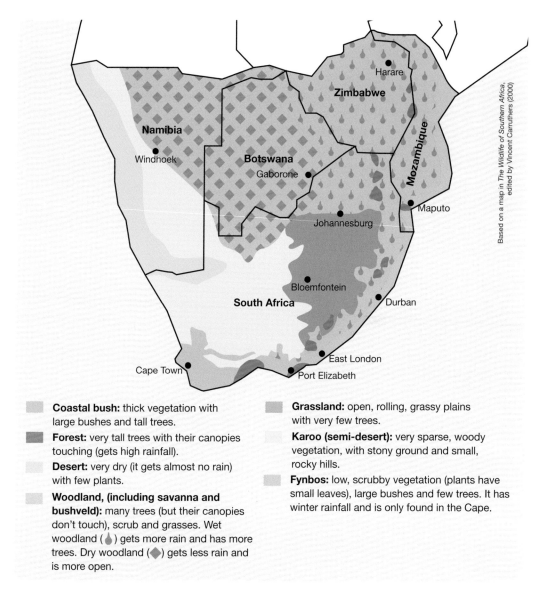

Based on a map in *The Wildlife of Southern Africa*, edited by Vincent Carruthers (2000)

Coastal bush: thick vegetation with large bushes and tall trees.

Forest: very tall trees with their canopies touching (gets high rainfall).

Desert: very dry (it gets almost no rain) with few plants.

Woodland, (including savanna and bushveld): many trees (but their canopies don't touch), scrub and grasses. Wet woodland (💧) gets more rain and has more trees. Dry woodland (◆) gets less rain and is more open.

Grassland: open, rolling, grassy plains with very few trees.

Karoo (semi-desert): very sparse, woody vegetation, with stony ground and small, rocky hills.

Fynbos: low, scrubby vegetation (plants have small leaves), large bushes and few trees. It has winter rainfall and is only found in the Cape.

Other common habitats, not on the map, include:

Gardens and parks: created by humans with grass, flowers, shrubs and trees.

Wetlands: habitats with water (see page 115 for more on wetlands).

Open fields and farmlands: created by humans for farming crops, such as maize and potatoes, and animals, such as cows and sheep.

Fancy feathers

What are feathers used for?

Birds have the amazing ability to fly. But they are not the only animals that can fly. Bats and insects can fly too. Birds are the only animals in the world that have feathers. Feathers have many uses.

Flying

Birds use their tough outer flight feathers to fly. These are found in the wings and tail. Flying has many benefits, like escaping from predators. Flying also allows birds to be swift, speedy hunters and to escape bad weather by migrating to other places.

A young **bateleur** stretches out its flight feathers.

Keeping warm

Birds have soft, fluffy feathers called down feathers. They grow close to the skin and keep birds from getting too hot or too cold. Young birds lose all their down feathers when they mature. Down feathers are used in human jackets, bedding and sleeping bags for warmth and comfort.

Very young birds only have down feathers, like the fluffy feathers of this young **spotted eagle-owl.**

Attracting a mate

During the breeding season, many male birds grow special breeding feathers that they use to display to the females. They are hoping to attract a mate. Read more about this on page 83.

How does a feather work?

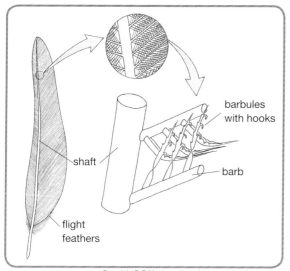

Copyright D G Mackean (www.biology-resources.com)

Every feather has hundreds of hair-like branches coming off a main stalk, called a shaft. The branches are called barbs. The barbs have smaller branchlets called barbules that cross over and fasten onto each other by small hooks. The barbules zip together to make a smooth, strong blade for flying. When feathers get ruffled and a bird preens itself, it is 'zipping up' its feathers. You can do it yourself with the feathers you find.

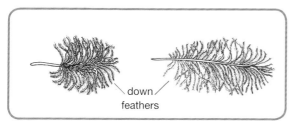

Down feathers don't zip up like flight feathers. They are loose and fluffy and trap air close to the body to insulate the body and keep it warm.

What are bristles for?

Some birds have short feathers surrounding their beaks. These are like stiff hairs and are called bristles. Most insect-eating birds have them. They guide the insect into the bird's mouth. If insects crawled over their eyes and face, the birds could be bitten or stung.

Square-tailed drongos, like many insect-eating birds, have bristles around their beaks.

Not all birds can fly. Some are adapted for running, such as ostriches, or for swimming, such as penguins. Flying birds all have strong, hollow bones. This keeps them light for flying. They also have powerful flight muscles.

Amazing adaptations

Adaptation means how an animal's body or behaviour changes over time so that it can survive better in its environment. Here are some amazing adaptations for finding food.

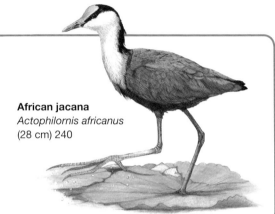

Who has the longest toes?

The African jacana has very long toes. They are the longest toes of any bird, compared to its body size. They are adapted to walking on floating plants on the water. The bird needs long toes to help it balance and to spread its weight so it doesn't sink.

African jacana
Actophilornis africanus
(28 cm) 240

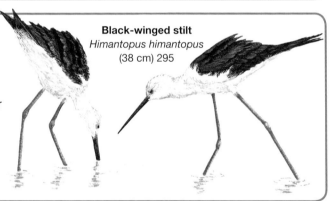

Who has long legs?

The black-winged stilt has the longest legs of any wader, compared to its body size. They are adapted to feeding in deeper water where other small waders can't reach.

Black-winged stilt
Himantopus himantopus
(38 cm) 295

To understand bird adaptations you need to ask some questions:

• What does the bird look like and what is it doing?

• Why do you think it needs to look or behave like that?

• How would these adaptations help the bird to survive better?

See some examples on pages 80–81 of how the shape of a bird's feet and beak help it to survive better.

Incredible journeys

Many birds migrate long distances every year. They migrate mostly to escape cold weather or find better food supplies. This amazing adaptation helps them to find better living conditions. In southern Africa, many birds come and go during the winter and summer months as they arrive in or leave the country.

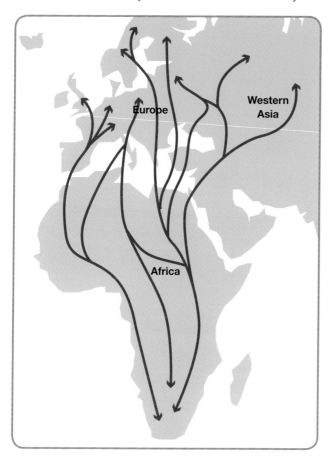

Europe

Western Asia

Africa

Humans have highways, birds have flyways!

This map shows many of the bird flyways from Europe and western Asia to Africa. Birds fly thousands of kilometres across deserts, mountains and seas and through storms. Humans are making their survival even harder because they are changing the face of the land through agriculture and chopping down indigenous forests. The birds are also hunted carelessly.

Migrating swallows

Barn swallows migrate between England and southern Africa twice a year! They travel up to 11 000 km to reach their destination! They arrive in southern Africa in the spring and spend the summer months feeding here. Then they leave in early autumn to return to England. It's springtime there and time to breed.

Barn swallow (European swallow) *Hirundo rustica* (14 cm) 518

Beak shapes

Birds must find food to survive. The shape of a bird's beak depends on what it eats.

Pink-throated twinspot

Seed-eaters, such as sparrows and twinspots, have cone-shaped beaks for cracking open seeds.

Tawny eagle

Eagles and owls have sharp, hooked beaks used for tearing the body of their prey into pieces small enough to swallow.

Spotted thick-knee

Birds with long, slender beaks are mainly insect-eaters. Their beaks are used to pick insects off the ground or from among leaves, twigs and bark.

Yellow-billed duck

Duck beaks are flattened and the edges are fringed to strain plants, seeds and small animals from mud and water.

Great white pelican

Pelicans have yellow pouches under their bills that stretch open like big nets when under the water. Fish are scooped up in the pouch.

Spot the different shaped beaks of the birds as you page through the book. Then read what they eat.

Feet shapes

The shape of a bird's foot tells you what kind of lifestyle it leads. Have a look below.

Perching birds, such as canaries and sparrows, have three toes pointing forwards and one pointing backwards. This is perfect for grasping perches or a branch.

Climbing birds, like woodpeckers and barbets have two toes pointing forwards and two backwards. They climb up, down and sideways on tree trunks.

Waterbirds, such as ducks and geese, have webbed feet for swimming.

Wading birds, such as herons and egrets, have long toes that spread out and stop them from sinking into the ground. Waders feed in shallow water where the ground is soft.

Raptors, such as eagles and owls, use their large talons to capture, kill and carry prey.

Groundbirds, such as guineafowl and chickens, use their strong feet to scratch in the dirt and leaf litter to find food.

Mandy Brockbank

Escaping predators

One of the biggest worries for birds, besides finding food, is to avoid being eaten! Birds have many different ways of doing this.

Safety in numbers

Many birds live in groups because there is safety in numbers. This means that one bird has less chance of being eaten in a group.

Red-billed quelea can gather in flocks of thousands of birds.

Defence tactics

Another reason for living in a group is group defence. This is when there are more eyes watching and the birds can warn one another of danger. The group also works together to fight off predators. For example, weavers mob snakes, hoping to chase them away from their nests.

Boomslang raid birds' nests for their eggs and chicks.

Camouflage

Many birds, like this **fiery-necked nightjar**, use camouflage to hide from predators. Its feathers are the same colour as the tree bark. The streaks and blotches on the feathers blend in with the texture of the bark. It sits lengthwise on the branch so that it becomes part of the tree. Its tail even looks like a branch and its beak could be a thorn.

Fiery-necked nightjar

Finding a mate

Flashy clothes

All birds want a chance to raise a family. But they have to find a mate first. They want a mate that is fit and healthy so their chicks will be fit and healthy too. It's usually the male birds that have to prove they are good enough for the females. Many male birds grow beautiful feathers, like flashy clothes, in the breeding season to attract females. These can be very elaborate, bright and colourful and sometimes extremely long!

Metamorphosis

The male **long-tailed widowbird** goes through metamorphosis in the breeding season. His colour changes from plain, streaky brown to pitch black, except on his wings. He also grows a large, long, black tail. He shows off to the females by flapping slowly over his territory in the grassland habitat with his long, heavy tail trailing behind.

breeding male

Long-tailed widowbird
Euplectes progne
(male: 60 cm including tail;
female: 20 cm) 832

non-breeding male

What is a territory?

Territories keep others out

Male birds usually set up a territory in the breeding season so they can attract a mate. A male bird sings to advertise his territory. If another male bird of the same kind arrives in his territory, he is chased off. Male birds have their territories next to one another and then compete for females. When a male bird sings to attract a female, he acts like an opera star! His singing becomes longer and more complicated. He is trying to sing better than his neighbour.

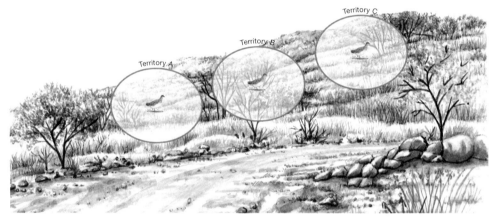

The territories of male birds usually lie next to one another. They don't overlap much. They don't share the space and food in their territories.

Do birds have more than one mate?

Many birds only have one mate at a time during the breeding season, like this **Cape batis**. This is called monogamy. Both parents help to build the nest and the male brings the female food while she keeps the eggs warm. Other birds, like weavers and cuckoos, do it very differently! Read pages 103 and 110.

Cape batis *Batis capensis* (13 cm) 700

Why do birds sing?

Birds need to talk

Birds need to 'talk' or communicate with one another. They sing to advertise their territories or to find a mate. Birds can hear one another over long distances because there is nothing to block travelling sound outside. They can also communicate in the dark and in thick vegetation without having to see each other.

Birds' calls are a great way to identify a bird. You don't even have to see the bird but you know it's there! Listen to all the different bird calls outside.

The **Cape grassbird** perches on a grass stem to sing and whistle.

How do birds sing?

The syrinx is the sound-producing organ in birds. Sound is produced when air from the lungs moves through the syrinx. Birds can control how loud or how long their song is by tensing the muscles of the syrinx. Birds with more muscles, like crows, starlings and parrots, can produce more detailed songs.

While a human's voice box is at the top of the air pipe or trachea, a bird's syrinx is at the bottom, close to the lungs. Air from the lungs goes to the syrinx through two tubes or bronchi. Each tube or bronchus makes its own sound. This means that a bird can sing two different notes at the same time.

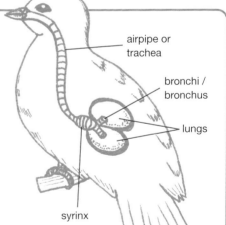

airpipe or trachea

bronchi / bronchus

lungs

syrinx

Parrots can talk because they have thick tongues like humans. Their tongue, throat and mouth change the sounds coming from the syrinx into words.

Conservation matters

Conservation is a way of looking after and taking responsibility for the natural world. Conservation came about because many animals and plants were disappearing from the Earth. Here are some of the problems.

Birds lose their homes

Humans are turning natural areas where birds live into towns, farms and exotic forests. Many birds, like cranes and blue swallows, can't survive without their natural habitat.

Exotic pine forests are replacing the habitats of many birds.

Birds are poisoned

Farmers use poisons on carcasses to kill jackals and other animals that harm their livestock. Vultures and some large eagles eat these poisoned carcasses and die. Farmers also use poisons on their crop seeds to protect them from pests. Many birds, like cranes (see page 93), eat the seeds and die. Other poisons used at home, such as slug bait and rat poison, kill birds living around us.

The **bearded vulture** (lammergeyer) lives in the high mountainous areas of the Drakensberg. This bird is endangered in southern Africa, mainly because they have been poisoned. A good way to identify this bird while it is flying is by its diamond shaped tail.

How can you help?

You can turn your garden into a place where birds want to live.

- Provide **water**. You can put out a birdbath or, even better, create a small pond that birds can visit.
- Provide **food**. The best way to do this is to grow a variety of plants in your garden that will provide different types of food: seeds for seed-eaters, fruit for fruit-eaters, insects for insect-eaters and nectar for nectar-feeders.
- Provide places to **nest** and **hide**. Plant shrubs and trees. Birds feel safer if they have somewhere to hide. You can also provide nesting boxes that you can buy at the hardware store or nursery.

Acacia trees, like this umbrella acacia, attract insects, which bring insect-eating birds. They also provide good nesting places.

Sugarbush flowers are rich in nectar and attract nectar-feeders.

The Umdoni waterberry attracts fruit-eaters with its red and purple fruit.

Seed-eaters are attracted to couch grass.

Be careful when using chemical poisons in the garden for killing pests and weeds. These affect other plants and animals. There are organic or natural products that are better to use.

▶ Groundbirds

Life on the ground

Groundbirds, such as francolin and guineafowl, spend most of their time on the ground. They find all their food on the ground and they nest here too. They are easy prey for snakes, mongooses, leopards and raptors, so they have adapted by using camouflage. Their feathers are plain, natural colours to blend in with the ground or vegetation. Predators then have a harder time finding them.

Alan Calenborne

Double-banded sandgrouse
Pterocles bicinctus (25 cm) 347
Using camouflage is one of the best ways to survive. Look how well this sandgrouse blends in with its surroundings.

The ostrich

The **ostrich** is definitely a groundbird. It can't fly! It is the world's largest and fastest running bird. It can run up to 70 kilometres per hour! It also lays the biggest eggs of all birds. Males have black feathers, while females are greyish-brown to blend in with their surroundings. The males are more concerned about looking handsome in black so they can attract a mate than they are about their safety.

male

female

Ostrich
Struthio camelus
(2 m) 1

Guineafowl

Beautiful feathered chickens

Guineafowl are like chickens in the way they feed. They scratch through the soil with their feet and dig around with their short, stout beaks. Like some other groundbirds, they have strong feet for walking on the ground. See the different feet shapes on page 81. They look for seeds and invertebrates to eat. They live in flocks when they are not breeding. Living in a flock helps with watching out for predators. One bird warns the others if it spots one. Large eagles and eagle-owls are guineafowls' enemies.

Helmeted guineafowl
Numida meleagris (56 cm) 203

Crested guineafowl
Guttera edouardi (50 cm) 204

Spot the difference

The two guineafowl on this page have different 'hair styles' and live in different places.

- The **helmeted guineafowl** has a bony 'casque' on top of its head, like a helmet, but no-one really knows what it's for. It lives in a wide variety of habitats, although it does prefer more open, grassy areas.
- The **crested guineafowl** has a curly, black crest on top of its head, like it's had a visit to the hairdresser. It is fussier and prefers thicker bush and forests to live in.

Read more about habitat specialists and generalists on page 74.

Do you know how birds cool down when it is too hot? They open their beaks and do gular fluttering! This is fast breathing in and out of the throat. In dogs, it is called panting.

Francolin and spurfowl

Birds with spurs

Francolin and spurfowl are groundbirds with curved beaks used for digging into the soil for bulbs and roots. The colours and patterns on their feathers are used for camouflage. This camouflage makes them look like part of their surroundings and makes it difficult for predators to spot them.

Francolin and spurfowl have tough, horny growths at the bottom of their legs called spurs. The males' spurs are particularly large and sharp. They use them for fighting with each other. They fight for territories during the mating season. Once a male has a territory, he has a better chance of finding a mate and raising some chicks.

Spot the difference

Francolin and spurfowl look very similar, but there are ways to tell them apart. Francolin are usually smaller than spurfowl. Francolin usually have yellow legs, while spurfowl usually have black, red or orange legs. Francolin prefer grassland habitat, while spurfowl prefer woodland habitat. Take a look at the habitat map on page 75.

Grey-winged francolin
Scleroptila africanus
(32 cm) 190

Natal spurfowl
(Natal francolin)
Pternistis natalensis
(34 cm) 196

Swainson's spurfowl
(Swainson's francolin)
Pternistis swainsonii
(36 cm) 199

How would you identify the birds on this page? Can you spot their differences?

Lapwings

Anti-predator tactics

Lapwings prefer to live in open places where there is little or no place to hide. This makes them easy prey for predators, especially as they spend most of their time on the ground. They also have to protect their nests, which are just shallow scrapes in the soil.

They have adapted by using some clever anti-predator tactics. The first is dive-bombing, which they do in pairs or groups. At the same time, they screech very loudly to frighten off the predator. This screeching is enough to raise the hairs on the back of your neck!

Lapwings also confuse predators by running away from their nests. Then they sit on the ground as though they are sitting on a nest. They have also been known to pretend to have a broken wing to distract a predator.

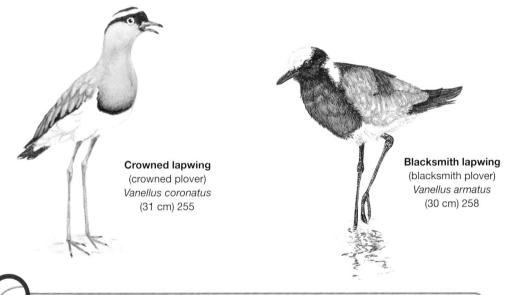

Crowned lapwing
(crowned plover)
Vanellus coronatus
(31 cm) 255

Blacksmith lapwing
(blacksmith plover)
Vanellus armatus
(30 cm) 258

Spot the difference

Crowned and **blacksmith lapwings** have different colouring and they live in different places.

- The crowned lapwing prefers short grass or bare areas, very often on sports fields or golf courses.
- The blacksmith lapwing prefers the shorelines of wetlands.
- The crowned lapwing eats termites and other insects.
- The blacksmith lapwing eats small invertebrates it finds on the shore.

Thick-knees

Birds with thick knees

Thick-knees get their name from the thickened knobs on their legs. These are actually their ankles, not their knees. In all birds, the bottom half of each leg is actually the foot. Thick-knees are active at night, when they hunt for insects on the ground using their long, slender beaks. They have large eyes for seeing in the dark. They have excellent camouflage. Eagle-owls (see page 129) are thick-knees' greatest enemy.

Spot the difference

If you spot a thick-knee and want to identify it, it helps to know what kind of habitat each one prefers. **Spotted thick-knees** prefer stony, open savanna or grassland, while **water thick-knees** prefer the banks of rivers, lakes, pans or dams. See the habitat map on page 75.

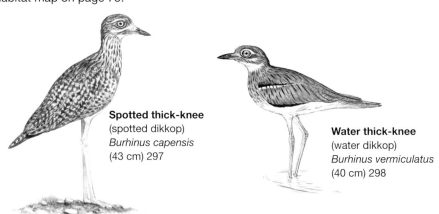

Spotted thick-knee
(spotted dikkop)
Burhinus capensis
(43 cm) 297

Water thick-knee
(water dikkop)
Burhinus vermiculatus
(40 cm) 298

Remarkable relationships

In the nesting season, a water thick-knee nests close to a crocodile's nest, usually on a sandbank. The crocodile protects the nest of the water thick-knee. In return, the bird makes loud, warning calls if there is danger, like a water monitor, nearby. Water monitors or leguaans are good at digging up the nests of crocodiles and eating their eggs.

A Nile crocodile

Cranes

Graceful birds

It's very special to see a crane in its natural habitat. They are lovely, tall birds with long legs and necks for walking and seeing above the grasslands and wetlands where they live. They have beautiful colours and markings and a train of tail feathers, which are really part of their wings. They are omnivorous, which means they eat plants and animals. The **blue crane** is South Africa's national bird.

Birds in trouble

Cranes are threatened by humans, especially the **wattled crane**, which is an endangered bird. Cranes are threatened because humans have put exotic forests and farms in their habitat. Humans also burn their habitat when they are nesting, which often kills the eggs and chicks. Humans do this for a number of reasons, such as getting rid of the old dry grass and to let new grass grow in its place. Cattle prefer fresh, green grass. Another problem is that the chicks are sometimes stolen from the nest and sold as pets.

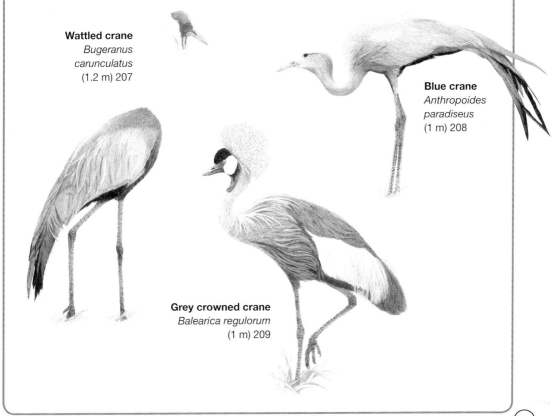

Wattled crane
Bugeranus
carunculatus
(1.2 m) 207

Blue crane
Anthropoides
paradiseus
(1 m) 208

Grey crowned crane
Balearica regulorum
(1 m) 209

▶ Passerines

More than half the birds in the world are passerines, so they are the biggest group of birds. Passerines are often called perching birds or songbirds as many of them perch or have lovely songs.

Perching birds

Passerines, like the **Cape sparrow**, are often called perching birds. They have three toes pointing forwards and one toe pointing back, and their toes are able to grip a branch. Ducks and geese are called non-passerines because they don't have a perching foot and find it very difficult to perch.

Ostriches are also non-passerines. They are the only birds in the world with two toes on each foot, so they definitely can't perch! But some perching birds are not passerines. Eagles and owls are non-passerines because, although they can perch, they have specialised feet with large talons used for hunting prey. See page 124.

female

male

Cape sparrow
Passer melandrus (15.5 cm) 802
Cape sparrows are passerines.
They can perch *and* sing.

Songbirds

Passerines are often called songbirds but not all of them can sing. Crows, for example, definitely can't sing although they do talk a lot! Canaries are passerines and lovely songsters. The males sing particularly well in the breeding season to advertise their territories and attract a mate. They sing using their syrinx, which is similar to a human's voice box. Learn more about this on page 85.

Cape canary *Serinus canicollis* (13.5 cm) 872
Cape canaries sing beautifully.

Pigeons

Two different pigeons, two different places

These two pigeons live and feed in very different places. The **speckled pigeon** lives on cliffs, rocky hills and buildings. It flies to open country to eat seeds and green shoots. In fact, some grain farmers don't like speckled pigeons because they eat all their seeds.

The **African green-pigeon** lives in dense woodland and forest. It lives off the fruit supplied by the trees. It is grey-green in colour, which helps to camouflage it among the leaves. When African green-pigeons are not breeding, they form flocks as an anti-predator strategy. Read more about this on page 82.

At night, pigeons roost together. Speckled pigeons roost and nest on the edges of cliffs or buildings. Green-pigeons roost and nest in trees. Read what roosting means below.

Speckled pigeon
(rock pigeon) *Columba guinea* (33 cm) 349

African green-pigeon
Treron calvus (29 cm) 361

Roosting is a bird's way of sleeping or resting. Birds roost in places where it's hard for predators to see or get to them. They roost alone or in groups. They sit down on their feet, tuck their heads in and fluff up their feathers. Roosting in a group helps the birds keep warm. There is also a better chance of one of the birds spotting a predator.

Doves

Common garden birds

Many birds are at home in our gardens and parks, like the **Cape turtle-dove** and **laughing dove**. You can recognise the Cape turtle-dove by the thin, black collar around the back of its neck. The laughing dove has a pinkish, spotty chest and no collar.

During the breeding season, when the males start looking for a mate, they can be very funny. They chase after the females, trying to impress them. During courtship they bow to the females with their necks puffed up. Like many birds, doves form mating pairs. They build a nest of twigs in the fork of a tree. The male and female share the job of building the nest, keeping the eggs warm and feeding the chicks.

Cape turtle-dove
Streptopelia capicola (28 cm) 354

Laughing dove
Streptopelia senegalensis (25 cm) 355

What's the difference?

- **Doves** feed on the ground. They eat seeds.
- Most **pigeons** feed in trees. They eat fruit.
- Doves are mostly smaller, with a shorter, rounded tail.
- Pigeons are mostly larger, with a long, squared-off tail.

Bulbuls

Chatty, busy birds

Bulbuls are very chatty, busy birds with yellow under their tails. They hop around branches or on the ground looking for food. They bounce and hop even faster and call 'chissik, chissik' if there is approaching danger, like a leopard, snake or owl. These are very useful warning signals for other animals and humans.

Spot the difference?

- The **Cape bulbul** has a white ring around its eye, which is how you tell it apart from the **dark-capped bulbul**.
- The Cape bulbul is endemic to the Cape fynbos, which means it is not found anywhere else.
- The dark-capped bulbul is found in woodland habitats, gardens and parks. Find these different habitats on the habitat map on page 75.

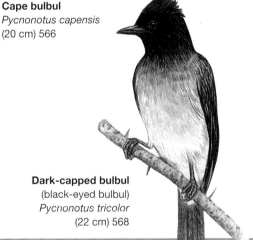

Cape bulbul
Pycnonotus capensis
(20 cm) 566

Dark-capped bulbul
(black-eyed bulbul)
Pycnonotus tricolor
(22 cm) 568

Rolf Wiesler

Helping plants

Bulbuls eat a lot of fruit, but also insects, nectar and seeds. They are important to plants because they spread their seeds. Bulbuls eat the fruit but don't digest the seeds. The seeds pass through their gut and out onto the ground. If the seed lands in a good spot, it will germinate and grow into a new plant.

Shrikes and puffbacks

Small hunters

Shrikes and puffbacks hunt prey from a perch or find prey among the leaves and branches of trees. They eat mainly insects, spiders and lizards, but the common fiscal (shrike) also eats mice, frogs and small birds. They have strong, hooked beaks, which they use for tearing food into smaller pieces.

Storing food

Common fiscals store their food by impaling it on a thorn or spike. This is called caching. Shrikes do this when food is short, but ornithologists also think they impale large prey to stop it escaping. It may also be a way of saying to a female: 'I am a strong, clever man who can catch lots of food!'

Common fiscal
Lanius collaris
(22 cm) 732

Family helpers

White-crested helmet-shrikes live in family groups, rather than alone or in pairs like some other shrikes. Each family member helps to incubate the eggs and feed the chicks. This improves the chances of the eggs and chicks surviving.

White-crested helmet-shrike
Prionops plumatus (18 cm) 753

A puffing display

During courtship, the **black-backed puffback** male displays to a female by puffing up his shiny white back or rump feathers. If she approves of him, they will mate, build a nest and help each other raise some chicks.

Black-backed puffback
Dryoscopus cubla
(18 cm) 740

Barbets

Plump little fruit-eaters

Barbets are plump little birds with large heads and thick, heavy beaks. The barbet's beak is well adapted for breaking open fruit and nuts and crushing insects. Barbets live in woodland habitats but are often found in gardens and parks and eat any fruit you leave out. They use their beaks for digging nest-holes in trees.

Make a wooden tray with a number of nails sticking into it. Then impale some old fruit or fruit skins on the nails. The barbets and other frugivores (fruit-eaters) will arrive for the feast!

Keeping territories

Like other birds, barbets sing to advertise their territories. This helps them keep other barbets of the same species out. They set up territories so they 'own' all the food, nesting and roosting sites in the territory. **Black-collared barbets** sing together. This song is called a duet. The male calls first, '*two*' followed by the female, '*puh-duh-ly*'. They say this 10 to 20 times. **Crested barbets** sound like alarm clocks: '*tr-r-r-r-r-r-r-r-r-r*'. It's easy to hear barbets!

Black-collared barbet
Lybius torquatus
(20 cm) 464

Crested barbet
Trachyphonus vaillantii
(24 cm) 473

Hoopoes and wood-hoopoes

Digging for food

Hoopoes and wood-hoopoes have long, slender beaks for probing or digging into or under something to find food. Hoopoes mostly dig for food in the ground, while wood-hoopoes mostly dig for food in trees, under bark or in flowers.

Favourite food

Centipedes hide in crevices or under the bark of trees during the day. They come out at night. Hoopoes and wood-hoopoes like to eat them, as well as insects and their larvae, geckos, lizards, frogs, fruit and nectar.

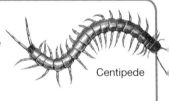

Centipede

African hoopoe
Upupa africana
(26 cm) 451

A bird that says its name

African hoopoes say their name when advertising their territory: 'hoo-poo', 'hoo-poo-poo'. They live alone, or in pairs when they are breeding. The pair nests in holes made by barbets and woodpeckers. Read about territories on page 84.

Cackling old women

Green wood-hoopoes live in family groups. They tell everybody where their territory is by cackling loudly together like old women. At the same time, they rock backwards and forwards together high up on a branch of a tree. They find natural holes in trees to nest in. The family helps to feed the mother and chicks, while she is looking after the eggs and raising the chicks.

Green wood-hoopoe
(red-billed wood-hoopoe)
Phoeniculus purpureus
(33 cm) 452

Starlings

What whistles and chatters in your garden?

Starlings often live in gardens or parks. If you don't spot their shimmering plumage, you may hear them chattering and whistling together. They are very sociable birds and get together in large, talkative groups. They have many muscles in their voice box, called a syrinx, so they can produce very complicated birdcalls. Read more about this on page 85. They can copy other birdcalls and even include other sounds, like sirens or car alarms, in their song. Starlings are omnivores: they hunt for insects on the ground but they also find fruit and nectar in the trees.

Spot the difference

- Many starlings, like the **Cape glossy starling**, are identified by their shimmering, blue-green colours. Glossy starlings prefer woodland habitats.
- **Red-winged starlings** are glossy, blue-black with red wings. They prefer rocky areas but often live around buildings and homes.
- Glossy starlings nest in holes in trees that other birds, like barbets and woodpeckers, have made. They even chase them off their nest-holes.
- Red-winged starlings make mud nests in crevices in rocks or on the rocky ledges of caves or buildings.

Cape glossy starling
Lamprotornis nitens (23 cm) 764

Red-winged starling
Onychognathus morio
(30 cm) 769

Weavers

Brilliant nest-builders

Weavers are brilliant nest-builders. They build or weave elaborate, dome-shaped nests that are never hidden away, but are obvious for all to see. There are three main weaver groups. The buffalo-weavers build stick nests, the sociable weavers build nests of dry grass, and the true weavers usually weave nests out of fresh vegetation. Buffalo-weavers are the only black weavers. They are named after their buffalo-like colouring! Weavers are seed-eaters with cone-shaped bills, although some species have more slender bills for eating insects.

Sociable weavers

Sociable weavers build giant communal nests made out of dry grass. They nest like this to control the temperature of the environment around them. They live in very dry or desert-like habitats where it's very hot in the day and very cold at night. At night they move deep into the central chambers of the nest, where the nest stays warm overnight. In the day, they use the outer chambers for shade. Sociable weavers use their nests all year round.

The giant grass nest of sociable weaver birds

Sociable weavers build the largest tree nests in the world. There can be up to 500 birds in one nest.

Sociable weaver
Philetairus socius
(14 cm) 800

David Mason (www.realbirder.com)

True weavers

True weavers, like **southern masked-weavers**, build nests by weaving and knotting grass and reed blades. It is amazing to watch! Male masked-weavers build a number of nests hanging from trees or upright reeds. Then they display to any females that may be watching under a nest they have built. They fan their wings and make a '*swizzle*' sound at the same time. If a female approves of a male and the nest he has built, they will mate and she will line the nest with grass, flowers and leaves. One male may have up to twelve nests at one time and will mate with many different females. This is called polygamy.

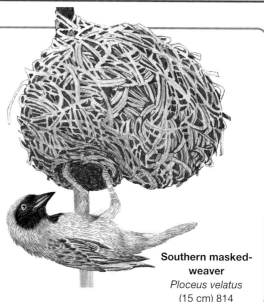

Southern masked-weaver
Ploceus velatus
(15 cm) 814

Buffalo-weavers

Red-billed buffalo-weavers build large communal nests out of thorny sticks in large trees. They use them all year round for roosting and nesting. See what roosting means on page 95. These weavers often nest over water because it is harder for predators like snakes to get to them. True weavers, like the masked-weaver, have attached their nests to the bottom of this buffalo-weavers' nest. The stick nests get so big vultures often nest on top of them.

Roger Broomhall

Red-billed buffalo-weaver
Bubalornis niger (21 cm) 798

Buffalo-weavers' stick nests are often built over water.

Sunbirds

Nectar suckers

Sunbirds are nectarivores or nectar-feeders. They suck sweet nectar from flowers. They have strong feet and sharp, curved claws for hanging onto the flowers while they feed. What is amazing is that they help many flowers with pollination, and without them many plants would not survive! They use their long, downward-curving beaks to get inside a tube-flower where other birds cannot go. The tongue forms a tube like a straw, which is used for sucking up the nectar.

Spot the difference?

There are 21 species of sunbird in southern Africa. Can you spot the difference between these three? Female sunbirds are always plain brown in colour, while the males are brightly coloured. She is trying to blend in with the environment to hide from predators, while he is trying to attract a mate. Read how male birds attract a mate on page 83.

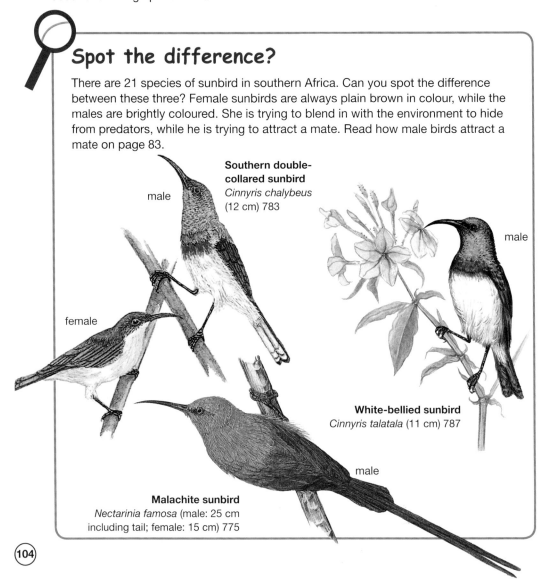

male

female

Southern double-collared sunbird
Cinnyris chalybeus
(12 cm) 783

male

White-bellied sunbird
Cinnyris talatala (11 cm) 787

male

Malachite sunbird
Nectarinia famosa (male: 25 cm including tail; female: 15 cm) 775

Kingfishers

Not all kingfishers eat fish

There are two groups of kingfishers: those that dive for fish and live close to water, and those that hunt other animals and live away from water.

Spot the difference?

The **brown-hooded kingfisher** lives away from water in dry areas, like woodlands and gardens. The **giant** and **pied kingfishers** live and nest close to water. Kingfishers hunt from a perch, scanning the ground or water for prey. Then they dive down to catch it in their beaks.

Brown-hooded kingfisher
Halcyon albiventris
(23 cm) 435

Giant kingfisher
Megaceryle maxima
(44 cm) 429

Pied kingfisher
Ceryle rudis (25 cm) 428
This kingfisher hovers over the water as it looks for fish to catch. Then it plunges headfirst into the water to catch the fish.

A very useful beak

Kingfishers have long, spear-shaped beaks, which are used for spearing and holding prey. The beak shape helps with accuracy – the bird looks down the length of its beak like it's looking down an arrow when aiming it at a target. They also use their beaks to dig holes into sandbanks where they nest. The holes can be one metre deep. They lay their eggs at the end of the tunnel.

Drongos and flycatchers

Insect-eaters with bristles

Drongos and flycatchers are insect-eating birds or insectivores. They perch on a branch while searching for prey. Then they shoot off the branch and catch the insect in flight or off the ground. Their beaks are used for catching and crushing insects and spiders. Around their beaks they have bristles, which are small, stiff feathers. They are used for feeling the prey and help to guide it into their mouths.

Spot the difference?

Drongos are easy to identify because they are totally black. The shape of the tail, either square or forked, tells you which drongo you have seen. The **fork-tailed drongo** prefers woodlands, while the **square-tailed drongo** prefers forests. See the habitat map on page 75.

Drongos are noisy, brave birds. They mob other birds, even large eagles and crows, if they get close to their nest or in their territories.

Fork-tailed drongo
Dicrurus adsimilis
(24 cm) 541

Square-tailed drongo
Dicrurus ludwigii
(19 cm) 542

African paradise-flycatcher
Terpsiphone viridis (male: 37 cm including tail; female: 17 cm) 710

The **African paradise-flycatcher** is a striking little bird with bright, chestnut-coloured wings and back.

The male stands out in the breeding season because he grows a lovely, long tail, like a streamer, to attract a mate.

Bee-eaters

Fast little flyers

Bee-eaters have adapted to feeding on bees and wasps, although they also eat butterflies, moths, beetles and dragonflies. They hunt from a perch. They have pointed wings and long tails, which make them very fast, agile flyers for catching their prey out of the air. Bee-eaters have long, pointed beaks for catching insects. Their beaks curve downwards so they do not block their view when they are hunting. They squeeze or rub prey on a branch to get rid of the sting.

Some birds get help

White-fronted bee-eaters nest in large groups, called colonies, in sandbanks. They dig tunnels up to one metre deep into the bank. They breed in family groups. The family helps to dig the tunnel and raise the chicks.

Little bee-eaters do not nest in colonies and don't have help raising their chicks.

White-fronted bee-eater
Merops bullockoides
(24 cm) 143

Little bee-eater
Merops pusillus
(17 cm) 444

Why don't perching birds fall out of trees when they sleep? When perching birds sit, a tendon on the back of the ankle contracts, locking their toes around the branch. With feet locked, sleeping birds don't fall. As the bird stands up, its feet release.

Ibises

Old men with hooked noses

Like the other bird groups, ibises have a particular shape that helps to identify them. They look a bit like old men with long, hooked noses! Their bills are very long and curve down for probing into soil or soft mud. The longer the bill, the deeper it can go. The tip of the bill can feel or smell for prey below the ground. Ibises have long legs for 'wading' through grasslands, which hadedas prefer, or through wetlands, which sacred ibises prefer. See the habitat map on page 75.

Ha..ha...Hadeda

The **hadeda ibis** says its name: 'Ha.. ha...Hadeda'. They call when there is danger to warn others. They dig deep into the ground for earthworms and king crickets. If you don't like king crickets, then hadedas are your friends! They also peck up insects, snails and lizards.

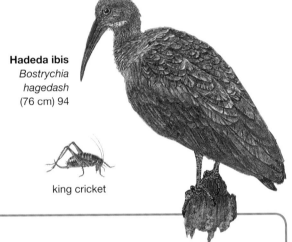

Hadeda ibis
Bostrychia hagedash
(76 cm) 94

king cricket

Living in groups

Sacred ibises are identified by their white and black colours. Like many birds they form flocks when they are not breeding. Living in groups makes it easier to spot predators and avoid them more quickly. Many eyes look out for danger and they warn one another if predators are nearby.

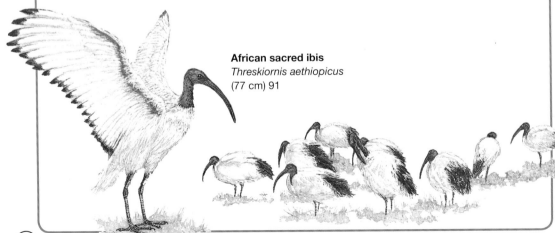

African sacred ibis
Threskiornis aethiopicus
(77 cm) 91

Hornbills and ground-hornbills

Hornbills are unmistakeable!

You can immediately identify a hornbill because of its very large, downward-curving beak! But which hornbill is it? Many hornbills have a casque (or 'helmet') on top of their beaks. The casque is usually hollow and is used to make their call louder.

Birds that sound like babies

Trumpeter hornbills have a very distinct call. They fly over the trees in groups, calling like crying babies: 'nha, nhaa ha ha ha'.

They look for fruit in the treetops.

Trumpeter hornbill
Bycanistes bucinator
(58 cm) 455

Whistling hornbills

Crowned hornbills have red bills with yellow at the base and their casque is small. They make loud, whistling calls.

They eat insects, other small animals and some fruit in trees or off the ground.

Crowned hornbill
Tockus alboterminatus
(52 cm) 460

A bird in trouble

Southern ground-hornbills are like large turkeys with red face skin and long, black eyelashes. They are groundbirds and don't fly much. See some other groundbirds on pages 88–93.

Ground-hornbills eat insects and larger prey, like hares, reptiles and frogs. But they are in trouble! Their populations are declining because humans are using their habitat for farming and they often kill them.

Southern ground-hornbill
Bucorvus leadbeateri
(1.1 m) 463

Cuckoos

Birds that never build a nest

Cuckoos have a very different way of raising their chicks. Can you believe they never build a nest but lay their eggs in other birds' nests when they are not looking? The other bird never seems to know the difference because she incubates the cuckoo's eggs and raises the chicks like her own! She is called the foster mother. Bulbuls, weavers, sparrows, sunbirds and drongos are examples of foster mothers. This behaviour of cuckoos is called **brood parasitism**. This means the female cuckoo is parasitising or harming the brood or clutch of eggs of the bird she lays her own eggs in.

The cuckoo mother may kick out an egg of the foster mother for every egg she lays. The cuckoo's eggs even look remarkably like the foster mother's eggs, in order to fool her. The cuckoo chick will also kick out any chicks or eggs of the foster mother's.

Why do cuckoos do this? So that they won't have to look after their own eggs but can continue laying more eggs in the hope that more of their chicks will survive.

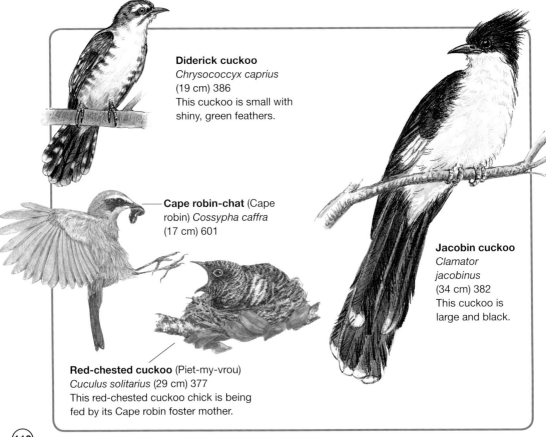

Diderick cuckoo
Chrysococcyx caprius
(19 cm) 386
This cuckoo is small with shiny, green feathers.

Cape robin-chat (Cape robin) *Cossypha caffra*
(17 cm) 601

Jacobin cuckoo
Clamator jacobinus
(34 cm) 382
This cuckoo is large and black.

Red-chested cuckoo (Piet-my-vrou)
Cuculus solitarius (29 cm) 377
This red-chested cuckoo chick is being fed by its Cape robin foster mother.

Woodpeckers

Tree climbers

Woodpeckers clamber up and down trees with their zygodactyl feet. They tap the branches and tree trunks to find tunnels where the larvae of beetles and other insects live. Then they dig open the tunnels with their chisel-shaped beaks. Their tongues are barbed for hooking onto the larvae and pulling them out of their tunnels. They also use their beaks for digging nest-holes into dead tree trunks. These provide nesting places for other birds, such as glossy starlings (see page 101).

Zygodactyl feet have two toes at the front and two at the back. They are well adapted for climbing. Barbets and parrots also have zygodactyl feet. See pages 99 and 113.

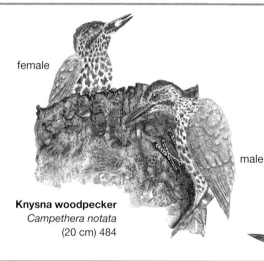

female

male

Knysna woodpecker
Campethera notata
(20 cm) 484

male

Cardinal woodpecker
Dendropicos fuscescens
(15 cm) 486

A different kind of woodpecker

Ground woodpeckers spend most of their time on the ground, unlike other woodpeckers. They prefer rocky hills and mountain places where they are well camouflaged among the rocks and boulders. They dig into cracks and holes in the ground with their beaks, looking for ant nests. Then they use their long, sticky tongue to lick up the ants and their eggs.

Ground woodpecker
Geocolaptes olivaceus (26 cm) 480

Turacos

Bright red flashes

Turacos, or louries, like to hide in the canopies of trees among the leaves. This is where they search for food. They have strong, curved beaks for breaking off and opening the leaf or flower buds and fruit they find on the branches. It's really hard to see them but sometimes, if you are lucky, they show themselves as they fly between the trees. It's easy to identify them because they have bright red wing tips that flash as they glide between the canopies.

Smart toes

Turacos can turn their fourth toe to the back so two toes point forwards and two toes point back. This allows them to move along the branches of trees easily without falling. They also use their beak for gripping. If they want to perch, the fourth toe moves to the front so they can grip a branch. See more about foot shapes on page 81.

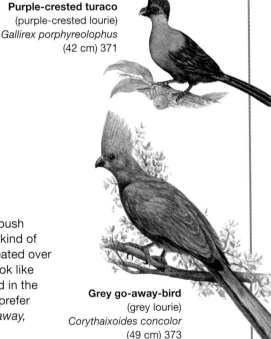

Purple-crested turaco
(purple-crested lourie)
Gallirex porphyreolophus
(42 cm) 371

Knysna turaco (Knysna lourie)
Tauraco corythaix (46 cm) 370

Spot the difference

The **turacos** on this page prefer dense bush and forest habitats. They have a similar kind of call – a loud, deep '*kor-kor-kor-kor*' repeated over and over again. **Grey go-away-birds** look like turacos but they are grey and only found in the northern parts of southern Africa. They prefer drier, woodland habitats. They say '*go-away, go-away*' from the tops of trees.

Grey go-away-bird
(grey lourie)
Corythaixoides concolor
(49 cm) 373

See page 75 to understand more about the different habitat types.

Parrots

Wild parrots

It's lovely to see parrots in the wild because we see them so often in cages. In the wild they are very gregarious, and live in flocks of up to 12 birds. **Cape parrots** prefer forests, while **brown-headed parrots** prefer woodlands, usually near water.

Parrots fly high, often above the tree canopies, between feeding and roosting or nesting places. They call as they go. Read what roosting means on page 95. Parrots eat mostly fruit but also seeds, nuts, flowers, green shoots and nectar. They have powerful, hooked beaks used for tearing the skin off fruit and crushing the hard shells of nuts and seeds. Their feet are zygodactyl, like woodpecker feet. This makes it easier to climb on tree trunks and branches. Read more about this on page 111.

Colleen Downs

Cape parrot
Poicephalus robustus
(34 cm) 362

Brown-headed parrot
Poicephalus cryptoxanthus
(23 cm) 363

Parrots nest in holes in trees, usually made by woodpeckers or barbets. The chicks stay in the nest for about 2 to 2½ months, while the parents bring them food.

There are fewer than 2 000 Cape parrots left in South Africa. The parrots like to nest in yellowwood trees and they prefer the fruit. But humans use yellowwood to make furniture, floorboards and boats, and are chopping down too many of the trees. Parrots are also stolen from the wild to sell as pets.

Broad-leaved yellowwood trees grow 10–30 metres tall.

Swallows and martins

Life in the air

Swallows and martins have adapted to feeding in the air. They are called aerial insectivores, which means they catch insects out of the air. They have short beaks that can open very wide. These act like small nets and prey is caught and swallowed whole.

They are superb fliers with long, pointed wings and forked tails, adapted to glide and manoeuvre easily. Swallows and martins often fly together in large flocks. Martins are much browner in colour. When breeding, swallows and martins pair off and build a nest of mud pellets stuck to a rock wall or building, or under a rocky overhang or roof.

Incredible journeys

Lesser striped and **blue swallows** are called intra-African migrants. They breed in southern Africa in summer. In winter they migrate north into Africa because it's warmer there and there is more food around. Some don't migrate at all if their home stays warm in winter. Barn swallows do it differently – they migrate to Europe every year. See them on page 79.

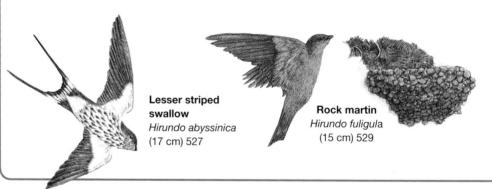

Lesser striped swallow
Hirundo abyssinica
(17 cm) 527

Rock martin
Hirundo fuligula
(15 cm) 529

A bird in trouble

Blue swallows are in trouble and may become extinct. They prefer mountainous grassland habitat with high rainfall. But most of their habitat has been taken over by exotic forest plantations. The trouble is they are habitat specialists, which means they prefer one kind of habitat and can't live anywhere else. Read more about this on page 74.

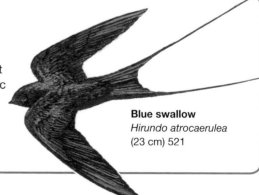

Blue swallow
Hirundo atrocaerulea
(23 cm) 521

▶ Waterbirds

What are waterbirds?

Waterbirds need wetlands to survive and breed. Examples of wetlands are rivers, streams, dams, ponds, swamps and waterholes.

Some waterbirds use wetland habitats to feed, roost and nest. Others, such as cattle egrets, only nest by the water and feed elsewhere. See page 118.

We have not included sea or estuary waterbirds in this book.

Marabou storks are mostly scavengers in woodland habitats but they will also hunt fish and frogs in shallow water (see also page 119).

Different kinds of waterbirds

Some waterbirds, such as ducks and geese, paddle in the water. Other waterbirds don't swim but perch over the water, such as fish-eagles. Some, like **yellow-billed storks,** wade into the water. Others use reeds and floating plants to walk on, such as African jacanas (see page 78). They all use different parts of the wetland and so avoid competing with one another for food and space.

This yellow-billed stork is fishing in the water. They hold their wings open to help them balance.

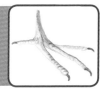

A wader is a bird that walks through the water, usually looking for food. Some waders have short legs and stick close to the bank, while others have long legs and can wade deep into the water. Their feet help them not to sink into soft ground.

Herons

Large waders

Herons are large waterbirds with long legs, long S-shaped necks and spear-shaped beaks. They can wade deep into the water with their long legs. They hunt alone, waiting patiently for prey to pass by or they stalk very slowly. Then their S-shaped necks shoot out when they spot prey, which is then grabbed by their long, spear-shaped beaks.

The spear shape helps with accuracy, like it does with kingfishers (see page 105). Herons eat fish, frogs, insects, reptiles, small birds and mammals. They nest in tall trees or reedbeds, often with other herons and egrets in large flocks. Look at the opposite page to learn more about heronries.

Goliath heron *Ardea goliath* (1.4 m) 64
This is the tallest heron, nearly the size of a small adult human.

Grey heron *Ardea cinerea* (1 m) 62

Black-headed heron *Ardea melanocephala* (92 cm) 63
They will also hunt in grasslands away from water.

Rolf Wiesler

What is a heronry?

Heronries are where certain waterbirds come together to nest in colonies. Cormorants, egrets, herons, spoonbills, darters and ibises are examples of such waterbirds. Often, many different species nest together in one colony, but sometimes one species will nest on its own. There can be just a few pairs or thousands of pairs nesting together. There is so much activity going on in these heronries that it's fascinating to just sit and watch them.

Anti-predator tactics

Heronries are usually found in large trees with spreading canopies that often hang over or stand in water. This protects them from ground predators, such as snakes, but not from aerial predators, such as eagles and crows. But there are many eyes that keep a watch out and they warn one another of any danger.

Roger Broomhall

This heronry consists mostly of cattle egrets. Read about egrets on page 118.

African spoonbills are waterbirds with spoon-shaped bills used for feeling in the water for small animals. They nest in heronries.

Egrets

White waterbirds

You can tell egrets apart from other waterbirds because they are so white. You tell the egrets apart from each other by looking at their size and the colours of their legs, feet and beaks.

The **cattle egret** is the only egret that is not a water wader. Instead, it wades through grasslands looking for insects. The other egrets hunt for fish and other animals in the water with their spear-shaped beaks. They hunt standing still, waiting for prey to pass by, or they stalk very slowly. Like herons, egrets hold their necks coiled back, ready to strike when they spot something to catch and eat.

Great egret
(great white egret)
Egretta alba
(95 cm) 66

Little egret
Egretta garzetta
(64 cm) 67

Great relationships

Cattle egrets form great relationships with large grazers, like cows and buffalo. They follow them through the grass and catch any insects that fly up when disturbed by their feet. Cattle egrets even perch on the backs of cattle in long grass to get a better view. All this helps the egrets to find more food. The cows and buffalo benefit because there are more eyes watching out for predators. The birds warn them of any danger.

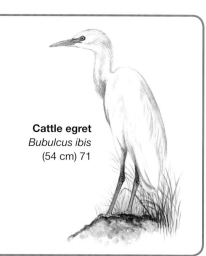

Cattle egret
Bubulcus ibis
(54 cm) 71

Storks

How do you identify a stork?

Storks are very tall birds with long legs and long, spear-shaped beaks. They are similar to the large herons (see page 116), but they don't have the heron's S-shaped neck and they fly with their necks stretched out. Most storks wade in water to find food, like the **saddle-billed stork**. They mainly eat fish, but also insects, crabs, frogs, birds and other animals. Marabou storks spend more time away from water. They are mainly scavengers and are found at carcasses or on rubbish dumps.

Saddle-billed stork
Ephippiorhynchus senegalensis (1.5 m) 88
This saddle-billed stork holds its wings open to help it to balance as it moves and lunges at prey.

Storks can't sing. Some of them are known to give raucous calls, squeaks or whistles. But they are mainly quiet because their syrinx muscles are very underdeveloped. Learn about what a syrinx is on page 85. They often communicate by snapping their bills open and closed to make a noise. This is called 'bill-clattering'.

Compare the two storks on this page to those on pages 74 and 115.

Scavengers

Marabou storks, like vultures, have naked, or featherless, heads and necks because they feed on carcasses. Any feathers would become clogged up with blood and goo when the birds put their heads inside a carcass.

Marabou stork
Leptoptilos crumeniferus
(1.5 m) 89

Alan Calenborne

Ducks and geese

Paddlers

Ducks and geese are paddlers. This means they float on top of the water like canoes. They use their webbed feet to push themselves through the water.

Ducks and geese are vegetarians. They eat seeds, stems, leaves, grass, and other plant parts. They feed by dabbling, which means they open and close their beaks at the surface of the water. Their beaks are flattened with a comb-like edge for filtering tiny food particles out of the water. They also graze grass in shallow water and **Egyptian geese** fly to grasslands or farmers' fields to graze. When not feeding, the birds rest on the shore.

Egyptian goose
Alopochen aegyptiaca
(68 cm) 102

Yellow-billed duck
Anas undulata (57 cm) 104

Many waterbirds, like ducks and geese, cover their feathers in an oil they get from the preen gland found under their tails. As you know, oil and water don't mix and always separate. You can try mixing them in a bowl at home to see what happens. Because of the oil, the water slides off the feathers and the ducks don't get wet.

Darters and cormorants

Swimmers

Darters and cormorants are swimmers. They swim very low in the water, much lower than ducks or geese. They check for fish and frogs by ducking their heads under the water. They are also divers because they swim right under the water to catch prey.

Unlike ducks and geese, which cover their feathers in oil, the feathers of cormorants and darters become soaked with water while swimming. After hunting, they sit with their wings open to warm their bodies and dry their wings. They have powerful, webbed feet for moving fast through the water and long, stiff tails that act like the rudder of a boat. These help to move them in whichever direction they want to go.

Spot the difference

- Darters have long, sharp beaks for spearing fish. They can swim with just their snake-like necks sticking out.
- Cormorants snap fish up in their beaks. Their beaks are hooked to stop slippery prey from escaping. They don't swim deep in the water like darters.

African darter
Anhinga rufa
(79 cm) 60

Reed cormorant
Phalacrocorax africanus
(55 cm) 58

Coots and moorhens

Walking on water

Coots and moorhens like wetlands with floating vegetation. For this reason, their toes are not webbed like ducks because they would find it awkward getting about on the vegetation. They also spend a lot of time paddling in the water during the day.

At night, they roost in bushes or reeds next to the water to hide from predators. They have short, stout beaks used for cutting through the water plants they feed on. They also eat seeds, berries, insects, tadpoles, crabs and snails. This means they are omnivores, as they eat plants and animals.

Different lifestyles

The toes of the **red-knobbed coot** are flattened into lobes, which help to push them through the water but still allow them to walk on floating plants.

They make a nest out on the water on floating plants. The parents cover the eggs with plant material to hide them.

The **moorhen** has long toes and legs for walking on vegetation around the water. They hide their nest in reeds or bushes above the water. The grey heron is a major predator of these birds. See page 116.

Red-knobbed coot
Fulica cristata
(43 cm) 228

Common moorhen
Gallinula chloropus
(34 cm) 226

Most waterbirds moult once a year. When they moult they lose all their flight feathers and new feathers are grown. During this time they can't fly, so they use deeper, open water to escape from predators or they gather in large groups for safety.

Small waders

Lovely small waders

There are so many lovely small waders, but we can only include a few of them here. Small waders have short legs and they wade through shallow water looking for food. Storks, herons and some of the egrets are the large waders with long legs. See them on pages 115–119.

Hammer-shaped heads

The **hamerkop** is a very interesting bird with a hammer-shaped head. It builds a massive nest of sticks and mud with nesting chambers on the inside. No one knows why it does this because it takes such a long time to build.

Hamerkop
Scopus umbretta (56 cm) 81

Three bands on their chest

Three-banded plovers are quick-moving little birds. They catch invertebrates with their slender beaks. They have two black stripes and one white stripe on their chests.

Three-banded plover
Charadrius tricollaris
(18 cm) 249

Escaping the winter

The little **wood sandpiper** escapes the winter in southern Africa by migrating to Europe and Asia. It's summer there so they go there to breed. They don't breed in southern Africa. When autumn arrives in Europe and Asia, they return to Africa as it's springtime here. They come here to feed in the summer months because it's warmer and there is more food around. Read more about bird migrations on page 79.

Wood sandpiper
Tringa glareola
(20 cm) 266

▶ Birds of prey

Large hunters

Birds of prey are carnivores and hunt live prey. They are also called raptors. The word 'raptor' comes from a word that means 'seize' or 'snatch' in Latin, because raptors seize prey with their strong feet and large, sharp talons. Examples of raptors are eagles, buzzards, kites, falcons and owls.

Their strong toes can kill their prey just by gripping and crushing it. Their talons may also kill the prey by piercing the soft tissue and organs. Raptors have powerful, hooked beaks with sharp cutting edges, used for tearing and cutting through the flesh.

The **secretarybird** is a bird of prey that hunts on the ground. It walks through open grasslands looking for insects, frogs, lizards, birds, small mammals, tortoises and snakes hidden in the grass. It kills its prey by striking down hard on it with its strong feet.

Secretarybird
Sagittarius sepentarius
(1.4 m) 118

Tawny eagle
Aquila rapax (71 cm) 132
Birds of prey, like this tawny eagle, hunt from a perch at the top of a tree or while flying.

Kites

Kite fliers

Kites are named after their habit of flying like kites in the sky. They hover high up with their heads still and wings flapping while they track their prey on the ground. Then they close their wings and swoop down onto the prey.

Yellow-billed kites don't hover. They sail through the air like kites blown by the wind. You can identify a yellow-billed kite by its forked tail when flying. The tail turns from side to side to help them manoeuvre through the air.

Some kites disappear in the winter

Yellow-billed kites migrate north to other parts of Africa during the winter months but breed here in the summer months. They migrate to find more food and escape our cold winters. **Black-shouldered kites** don't migrate. They stay in southern Africa all year round.

Black-shouldered kite *Elanus caeruleus*
(30 cm) 127
They mainly eat rodents, such as striped mice, but also insects, lizards and small birds.

Yellow-billed kite
Milvus aegyptius
(55 cm) 126b

striped mouse

The highest-flying raptor was recorded at 30 000 feet. That's 9 km high! We know this because an aeroplane struck it. Most raptors are big and bulky and use thermals, which are rising air currents, to soar and glide. In this way they don't have to flap their wings and use up too much energy.

Buzzards

What is a buzzard?

Buzzards are stocky, medium-sized raptors with broad wings. They either hunt from a perch or they swoop down over the habitat, scanning the ground for prey. They eat small mammals such as rodents and hares, snakes, lizards, insects, frogs and birds.

Spot the difference

Steppe buzzards prefer to live in open woodland, grassland and farming areas.

They are called non-breeding, Palaearctic migrants. This means they migrate to Europe and Asia to breed there in summer. When winter arrives in Europe, they migrate back to Africa because it's summer in Africa and there is more food around. They don't breed here.

Steppe buzzard
Buteo vulpinus
(48 cm) 149

Jackal buzzard
Buteo rufofuscus
(50 cm) 152

Jackal buzzards like hilly and mountainous habitats. They are often spotted as they soar or hover over valleys and mountainsides, or perch on rocks and telephone poles. They stand out more than other buzzards because they have reddish patches on their chests.

They don't migrate. They start breeding in October when the weather is warm and there is plenty of food around.

Eagles

Powerful raptors

Eagles are large, powerful raptors. They have long, broad wings and massive feet. They hunt bigger prey than other raptors because they themselves are so big. Examples are monkeys, baboons and dassies. Eagles live in different habitats so they avoid competition with one another. Birds compete for food and living space. There is only so much available in a habitat.

Spot the difference

Crowned eagles live in forests or dense woodland. They soar over the forest looking for prey. Once prey is heard or spotted, the bird lands on a perch and waits for the right moment to launch a surprise attack.

African crowned eagle
Stephanoaetus coronatus
(85 cm) 141

Martial eagles are the largest African eagles. They prefer open savanna and woodlands. They hunt mostly in flight, circling high above their territory, before swooping down in a shallow dive to catch prey by surprise.

Martial eagle
Polemaetus bellicosus
(81 cm) 140

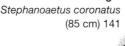

Savannas, woodlands and forests are examples of different types of habitats in southern Africa. Find these habitats on the habitat map on page 75.

Eagles that prefer rocky cliffs

Verreaux's eagles live in mountains and rocky places, especially on large cliffs. They soar across the cliff face, taking prey by surprise. They mostly eat dassies, because they share the same habitat. Like other raptors, pairs mate for life. They build stick nests on the edge of rocky cliffs, where they are hard to reach and safer from predators. They use the same nest site year after year.

Verreaux's eagle (black eagle)
Aquila verreauxii
(88 cm) 131

Dassies are a favourite food of the Verreaux's eagle.

Eagles that prefer water

Fish-eagles live around wetlands and are also waterbirds. Read more about waterbirds on pages 115–123. They perch high up in tall trees overlooking the water. They snatch fish with their sharp talons near the water surface or by dive-bombing into the water. They have small hooked scales under their feet for better grip on the slippery fish.

Fish-eagles also eat other waterbirds, raid their nests for eggs and chicks, and steal the fish they have caught. They are a danger to heronries. Read more about heronries on page 117.

African fish-eagle
Haliaeetus vocifer
(68 cm) 148

Siblicide occurs in Verreaux's and crowned eagles. The mother lays two eggs in her nest but only one survives! This is because the older, stronger chick, which usually hatches first, kills the younger, weaker chick. This is called siblicide.

So why lay two eggs? The eagle lays two eggs because it gets a second chance with another egg. One egg may not hatch or could be eaten by predators, or the older chick may die.

Owls

Nocturnal birds of prey

Owls are nocturnal birds of prey, which means they are active at night. They hunt nocturnal animals that use night-time to hide from the many daytime predators.

Owls have amazing adaptations for nocturnal hunting. They have very large eyes with big pupils for seeing in the dark and incredibly sharp hearing for locating prey without having to see it. They can fly so silently that prey can't hear them coming. They can also turn their heads all the way around to the back without having to make any noise with their bodies.

Verreaux's eagle-owl (giant eagle owl)
Bubo lacteus (62 cm) 402
This owl has pink eyelids.
It is one of the largest owls.

Hidden hunters

The **spotted eagle-owl** has two large, yellow eyes and obvious ear tufts. The ear tufts are not actually part of its ears but are thought to help with camouflage. It lifts its ear tufts when disturbed to break the outline of its body. This helps it to blend in with its surroundings.

It hunts from a perch, hidden in the dark. When it hears or sees prey, it drops down to catch it with its powerful feet. Learn about the feet shape of birds on page 81.

Alan Calenborne

Spotted eagle-owl *Bubo africanus* (45 cm) 401

▶ Scavengers

Vultures

Vultures are scavengers, which means they eat carcasses. By scavenging, they clean up the veld and prevent the spread of disease.

They glide and soar at great heights, searching for carcasses below. Most of them are big and bulky and use thermals for soaring and gliding. The higher they fly, the further they can see. They have exceptional eyesight for spotting, and large broad wings for soaring. They have long necks for probing into carcasses and hooked beaks for tearing and picking at the remains.

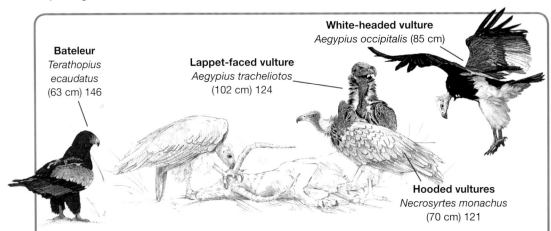

White-headed vulture
Aegypius occipitalis (85 cm)

Bateleur
Terathopius ecaudatus
(63 cm) 146

Lappet-faced vulture
Aegypius tracheliotos
(102 cm) 124

Hooded vultures
Necrosyrtes monachus
(70 cm) 121

Competition at a carcass

Bateleurs are raptors but they often scavenge like vultures. See page 124 for more about raptors. Bateleurs often spot a carcass first.

Hooded vultures are small vultures. They can't compete with the other vultures so they take meat away from the carcass. They also pick up scraps dropped or left behind.

White-headed vultures often find a carcass first. They are forced to give up feeding if large numbers of white-backed vultures arrive, because the white-backed vultures are larger than them. White-headed vultures also hunt small mammals.

The **lappet-faced vulture** is the largest vulture and can chase other vultures away. It often arrives last at the carcass and feeds on the tough skin and ligaments that other vultures can't manage.

The necks and heads of vultures are sparsely feathered or bald so that the blood and grime has nothing to stick onto. What does stick can be easily washed away in water.

The strongest wins

White-backed vultures usually follow other scavengers to the carcass. They live in groups and can chase off smaller vultures. They need a carcass to be opened so they can feed on the softer tissues. A large group of them can eat a dead impala in 10 minutes. They eat as fast as possible because they are chased away by stronger animals, such as jackals and hyenas.

White-backed vultures
Gyps africanus
(95 cm) 123

Helping birds in trouble

Many vultures are in trouble because they have lost their main food supply, which are the carcasses or the bodies of dead animals. Humans have killed many large carnivores, such as lion and leopard, which leave carcasses in the veld. Some nature reserves and farmers help by setting up vulture 'restaurants' where they throw their dead animals. This benefits the farmers *and* the vultures.

Frogs and Reptiles

▶ All about frogs and reptiles

Getting to know frogs and reptiles

Frogs and reptiles aren't always everybody's favourite animals! Yet once you understand them beyond just what they look and feel like, you will find them fascinating. The dry, scaly skin of reptiles and wet, slimy skin of frogs are adaptations to survive in their environment. You can read more about this on pages 152, 153 and 164.

Unlike mammals and birds, which are warm-blooded, reptiles and frogs are both cold-blooded. Yet they lead very different lives. Reptiles live mostly on land, while frogs live double lives in water and on land. Frogs and reptiles eat thousands of insects and small mammals, which would otherwise multiply into millions, every day. But they too have to avoid becoming food for other predators.

In this book we will introduce you to some of the more common kinds of frogs and reptiles you can find in southern Africa. We will also explore many of the amazing adaptations and habits they have developed in order to survive in their environment.

Deon Guyt

A southern tree agama

The value of frogs and reptiles

They are a link in the food chain

A food chain is how all living things depend on one another as food to survive. For example, frogs eat a huge number of insects. Frogs in turn are food to many other animals, such as fish, lizards, snakes and birds. Snakes are food to animals such as jackals, genets, civets, mongooses, wild cats, honey badgers, even leopards and other snakes.

The example below shows a very simple food chain. Without the frog and snake as a link, this food chain would break down.

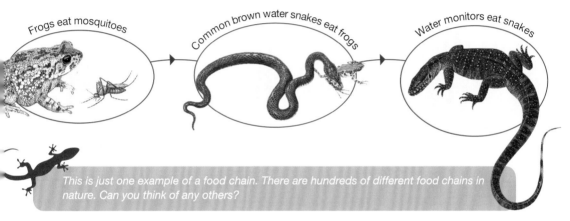

Frogs eat mosquitoes

Common brown water snakes eat frogs

Water monitors eat snakes

This is just one example of a food chain. There are hundreds of different food chains in nature. Can you think of any others?

A balance in the ecosystem

An ecosystem is made up of plants and animals living together. They interact and work together in a way that makes sure the whole system survives. Frogs and reptiles help to keep a balance in the ecosystem by feeding on insects and other animals. Here are some examples:

- Frogs eat millions of insects and help to control their numbers.
- Snakes control the numbers of rats, mice and dassies.
- Lizards, like geckos and chameleons, eat flies, mosquitoes, cockroaches and other insects that are pests in our homes.

Flap-neck chameleons eat flies and mosquitoes, which are pests in our homes.

135

The science in a name

Every frog and reptile is given its own Latin (or scientific) name and common (or English) name. The Latin name is used all over the world. It is written in italics. Italic letters slope to the right, *like this*. The common name can vary from country to country. Look at the example below.

The study of frogs and reptiles is called herpetology. A scientist who studies frogs and reptiles is called a herpetologist.

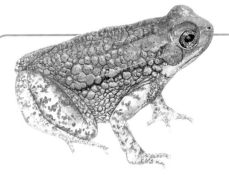

Latin name: *Schismaderma* is the genus name and is like a person's surname, e.g. Sekati. The second word, *carens*, is the species name and is like a person's first name, e.g. Peter.

Common name: This is the name most people use.

Red toad *Schismaderma carens* (7–9 cm)

This is the length of the animal, written in metres (m) or centimetres (cm). For frogs the length is measured from the tip of the nose to the end tip of the body (the legs are excluded). For tortoises and terrapins the length of the shell is measured. For snakes, lizards and crocodiles, the length is measured from the tip of the nose to the tip of the tail.

There is a huge diversity of frogs and reptiles in southern Africa. There are about 130 frog species and about 710 species of reptiles, of which 517 species are lizards; 146 species are snakes; 28 species are chelonians (which include 14 tortoises, 9 terrapins and 5 sea turtles); 18 species are worm lizards; and one is a crocodile.

Classification helps identification

When we classify a frog or reptile, we put it into groups with other animals that have the same or similar features. This helps us identify it.

Frogs and reptiles in the same group are similar – they are like one another. Frogs and reptiles in different groups are different – they are unlike one another. Examples of group names are Genus, Family, Order, Class, Phylum and Kingdom.

To give you an idea of how this works, this is how the red toad, *Schismaderma carens*, is classified:

Kingdom	**Animalia**	This group includes all the animals. Another kingdom would be Plantae, or plants.
Phylum	**Chordata**	This group includes all the vertebrates or animals with a backbone.
Class	**Amphibia**	This group includes all frogs, salamanders, newts and caecilians. If we were classifying a reptile species, the class name here would be Reptilia.
Order	**Anura**	This group includes all the frogs.
Family	**Bufonidae**	This group includes all true toads.
Genus	***Schismaderma***	The red toad is the only toad in this group.
Species	***Schismaderma carens***	This is the red toad.

The more specific the classification, the more similar the animals are to others in the group. For example, the toads grouped in the **family** Bufonidae are more similar than the frogs grouped in the **order** Anura. And these are more similar than the frogs, salamanders, newts and caecilians grouped in the **class** Amphibia.

This system of classification is used all over the world. It's a way to identify and share the information about all the plants and animals found on Earth.

Habitats are home

What is a habitat?

Frogs and reptiles are found in many different kinds of habitats. A habitat must provide them with all the things they need to survive, such as food, water and shelter. Examples of habitats in southern Africa are grassland, forest, desert, fynbos, karoo (semi-desert), savanna and coastal bush.

D. Gwynne-Evans

A habitat is defined by its particular kind of climate (weather), geology (type of rocks found there), topography (the surface features of an area) and group of plants and animals.

Angulate tortoises live in the Cape in South Africa. They prefer fynbos and karoo habitats.

Favourite places

Animals have particular places they prefer to live within a habitat. Examples are pans, ponds, reed beds, rivers, rocks, mountains, trees, open ground or underground. If we learn about these favourite places, it helps us to understand and identify them.

Kevin Drummond-Hay

Gonzalo Aguilar

This **southern spiny agama**'s favourite place is on the ground, where it digs tunnels for shelter and protection from predators. It is found in karoo and very dry savanna habitats.

This **southern rock agama**'s favourite place is on rocks and it will find a hole or crack in the rocks for shelter and protection from predators. It lives in many kinds of habitats, but not desert.

Habitat preferences

Some animals can only live in one or two different kinds of habitats. They are called habitat specialists. Others can live in many different kinds of habitats. They are called habitat generalists. Habitat generalists, like **puff adders**, usually survive better than habitat specialists, like **gaboon adders**, because they are more adaptable.

Jelger Herder

Jelger Herder

Puff adders live right across southern Africa. They live in many different kinds of habitats, except desert, thick forest or the tops of mountains.

Gaboon adders are only found in particular habitats. They prefer thick coastal bush and mountain forests. They are threatened because their habitat has been destroyed by the planting of exotic forests, tourist development and the mining of sand dunes.

We can actually use the shape of a frog's foot to help us identify it. This is because different species live in different habitats and have adapted in different ways. Herpetologists also look at the shape of a frog's pupils to identify it! Read more at the bottom of page 158.

Jelger Herder

Reed frogs have sticky pads under their toes for climbing up plants. Frogs that live in water have webbed feet for swimming, like the platanna on page 154. Toads and sand frogs have special hard ridges on their heels for digging. Have a look on page 157.

Cold-blooded animals

The correct word is 'ectotherms'!

Frogs and reptiles are known as cold-blooded animals. This does not mean that their blood is cold but that they cannot control the temperature of their own bodies. Their body temperature changes with the surrounding temperature. If it is hot, they are hot. If it is cold, they are cold.

The correct word for this is 'ectothermic', which means 'outer warmth'. To warm up, reptiles bask in the sun. To cool down, they move into the shade.

Marco Pauw

This **southern spiny agama** is basking on a bush. It is well camouflaged. This helps protect it from predators.

Many animals, like **crocodiles**, open their mouths to cool down, which is like a dog panting. Moisture evaporates through their open mouths, which cools down the blood in their bodies.

Warm-blooded animals

Mammals and birds are warm-blooded animals. The correct word for this is 'endothermic', which means 'inner warmth'. They keep the same body temperature no matter what the surrounding temperature is in the environment.

The advantage of being an ectotherm is that they don't need to eat very often. Some snakes only eat 10 meals a year! Mammals and birds need to eat every day. They turn food into body heat to keep warm.

Amazing adaptations

Adaptation means how an animal's body or behaviour changes over time so that it can survive better in its environment.

Surviving when it's too cold or too hot

Being cold-blooded, frogs and reptiles have a problem in areas where it gets very cold in winter because they have a hard time keeping warm. They have adapted to the cold weather by going into a hibernation-like state. This means they go into a resting, sleeping state in the winter.

Frogs and reptiles hide in any hole they can find, hide in thick vegetation or dig their own holes, such as **yellow-throated plated lizards**. They can hide for six months or more. Some frogs and reptiles also 'hibernate' when it's hot in summer, such as **bushveld rainfrogs**

Reptiles would cook if the temperature got too high and frogs would dry out.

Lesley Henderson

Jelger Herder

Yellow-throated plated lizards dig burrows to live in. They also use them to 'hibernate' in during cold weather.

Bushveld rainfrogs are only seen for a very short time in the rainy season. The rest of the time they 'hibernate' under the ground.

Changes during 'hibernation'

- The animals' body temperature drops to match the surrounding temperature.
- Their heartbeat and breathing slow down. For example, the heartbeat of a crocodile drops to about two to three beats per minute!
- They don't eat, but live off stored body fat. Crocodiles live off the stored fat in their tails.
- Their bodies almost shut down. They don't seem to see, hear or feel things going on around them.
- They hardly move at all.

Finding food

How do frogs eat?

Frogs are carnivores, which means they are animal-eaters. They eat insects, spiders, worms, snails, slugs, fish, small rodents like mice and even each other. Frogs have large eyes for seeing prey at night because this is when they hunt for food.

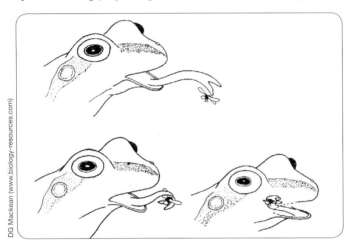

DG Mackean (www.biology-resources.com)

When a frog spots a tasty meal, it flicks out its long, sticky tongue. The flick of the tongue happens in the blink of an eye! It pulls its tongue back into its mouth with the prey stuck on. Platannas are frogs without a tongue. Read how they catch their prey on page 154.

Wide mouths and no teeth

Frogs have very wide mouths because they swallow their food whole. They don't chew their food because most of them don't have teeth for chewing. Some frogs, like bullfrogs (on page 163), have small teeth at the front for holding or biting onto large prey so that they can't escape.

Louis du Preez

This **guttural toad** is swallowing another frog!

Eyeballs help!

A frog uses its eyeballs to help it swallow its prey! This is because a frog's tongue is positioned at the front of its mouth and can't help with swallowing. When a frog swallows large prey, it blinks. This pushes its huge eyeballs down on top of its mouth. Together the tongue and eyeballs squash the prey and push it down the frog's throat.

How do reptiles eat?

Most reptiles are carnivores, although some are herbivores, like most tortoises, and others are omnivores, like some lizards. Reptiles have no teeth to chew their food so they swallow food whole or rip it off in chunks. Here are a few of the amazing adaptations some reptiles have for eating.

Double-jointed jawbones

Many snakes swallow very large prey, much bigger than their mouths. They can do this because their jawbones are flexible and loosely connected to each other. The lower jaw can shift right out of its normal position and the two halves that make up each side of the jawbone can separate and move on their own!

Shannon and Kay Clark APSSA

This python has caught a bushbuck and is swallowing it whole. Learn more about pythons on page 187.

Fast, speeding tongues

A **chameleon** hunts by shooting out its long, sticky tongue. The tip of the tongue is shaped like a club and covered in sticky mucus so the prey sticks to it. The tongue can also stretch longer than the length of the chameleon's body. Imagine if a human's tongue could do that!

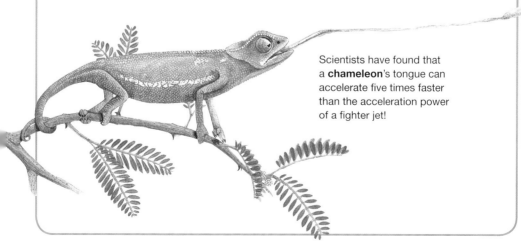

Scientists have found that a **chameleon**'s tongue can accelerate five times faster than the acceleration power of a fighter jet!

Escaping predators

How do frogs escape predators?

In order to survive, frogs have to escape the many predators that want to eat them. They use different anti-predator tactics to do this.

Frog camouflage

Most frogs use camouflage to hide from predators. They are mottled, blotchy or patchy in muddy-browns or green colours.

This helps them blend in with their surroundings. Some can even change their colour to match the background.

Jelger Herder

Can you spot this **foam nest frog**? Read about this frog on page 161.

Alarming tactics

Some frogs use a warning call or alarm call, like screaming noises or large grunting noises. They also try to frighten off predators by blowing themselves up, like **bushveld rainfrogs**, or lifting themselves up onto their legs to look bigger, like **banded rubber frogs**.

This **bushveld rain frog** will blow itself up into a hard, round ball to threaten predators.

Poison warnings

Frogs use bright colours, like reds, blues and yellows, to warn predators that they are poisonous to eat. The **banded rubber frog** has red and black stripes. Toads have poison glands behind their eyes that put off predators. Have a look at these on page 156.

The **banded rubber frog** is brightly coloured.

There are no poisonous or dangerous frogs in southern Africa that can harm humans.

How do reptiles escape predators?

Reptiles also have to escape predators to survive. As you will see below, many of the anti-predator tactics they use are very similar to those used by frogs.

Reptile camouflage

Reptiles have colours and patterns on their skin that blend incredibly well with their surroundings. **Gaboon adders** are beautiful snakes that blend in well with the leaf litter lying on the forest floor, which is where they live. They also use this camouflage to ambush their prey.

Gaboon adder
Bitis gabonica (80–120 cm)

Self-defence

Most reptiles give a warning sign first if they feel threatened. The **rinkhals** rears up and spreads its hood to warn an enemy. If this does not work, it can spray its venom up to two metres at the enemy's eyes.

hood

'**Rinkhals**' means 'banded neck' in Afrikaans. It was given this name because of the white bands on its neck.

Body armour

Many reptiles use body armour to protect themselves, like tortoises use their shells. Girdled lizards, like the **armadillo girdled lizard**, have spiny scales on their bodies for protection. It will roll into a tight ball, making it too spiny for predators too eat.

The **armadillo girdled lizard** is threatened because it is often collected illegally to be kept or sold as a pet. Read how you can help on page 151.

Justin Maguire

Finding a mate

Part of survival means finding a mate. In most frog and reptile species, the male has to attract a female and also fight for her.

Calling all females

The rainy season is the mating season for frogs. Male frogs call to the females of their own kind and females will not respond to any other frog species. The strongest male frog usually has the loudest call. The louder he calls, the better chance he has of attracting a female.

A frog, like this **Tinker reed frog**, has an elastic pouch under its throat, called a vocal sac, which blows up like a balloon when it calls. The vocal sac acts like a resonance box, which makes the call incredibly loud.

May the best frog win

Male frogs compete with each other for females. They each choose a special position from which to call to the females.

The strongest frogs get the best positions. They give a warning call to other males to keep away. If another male intrudes into his space, he will be attacked. He can be pushed, wrestled and kicked! The loser will move off.

Two male **Natal tree frogs** fight for a mate during the breeding season.

Flashy colours

Some male reptiles have to prove they are worthy mates by 'dressing up' in flashy colours. They usually have to compete with other males to win a mate.

Lizards with flashy colours

A male agama, such as this **southern tree agama**, develops bright colours in the breeding season to attract a mate.

He will use his bright colours to display himself and as a warning to other males to keep away. If another male challenges him, they will fight. They lash out at each other with their tails and threaten each other with their jaws open. They might have to wrestle and bite until one runs away.

A male **southern tree agama**'s head and throat go brighter blue in the breeding season. He displays to the females by bobbing his head.

Lesley Henderson

Snakes can dance

Female snakes leave a scent trail for males during the mating season.

More than one male may find a female and some will compete for her. They do this by wrestling with each other. First they raise and twist their upper bodies. Then they try to push each other's neck to the ground. This is called combat dancing. Eventually one of them, usually the younger or weaker one, moves off, and the winner claims his mate.

During the mating season a male **boomslang** follows the scent trail left by the female until he finds her.

Miles Veysey

The best way of finding or identifying frogs is by their call. Each frog species has its own unique mating call. You can track down frogs at night but you will need a good torch and loads of patience. Remember to wear your gumboots!

Learning about lifecycles

The lifecycle of frogs

A lifecycle describes the stages or changes an animal goes through as it develops from an egg to an adult. Frogs develop through complete metamorphosis. The tadpoles look completely different from the adults. While we never see the changes butterflies and moths go through inside their pupa or cocoons, we can actually see tadpoles slowly and gradually changing into frogs!

> Another name for all frogs and toads is amphibians. 'Amphibious' or 'amphibian' means 'double life' because these animals live on land and in water.

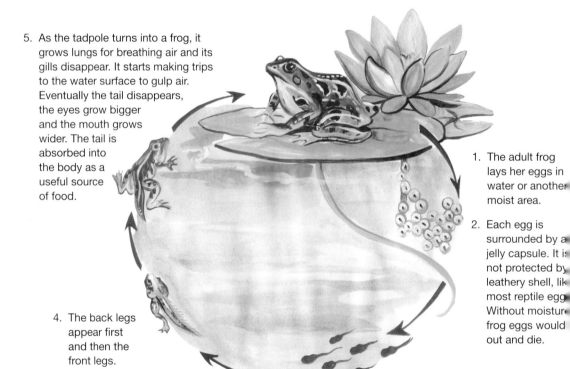

5. As the tadpole turns into a frog, it grows lungs for breathing air and its gills disappear. It starts making trips to the water surface to gulp air. Eventually the tail disappears, the eyes grow bigger and the mouth grows wider. The tail is absorbed into the body as a useful source of food.

1. The adult frog lays her eggs in water or another moist area.

2. Each egg is surrounded by a jelly capsule. It is not protected by a leathery shell, like most reptile eggs. Without moisture frog eggs would out and die.

4. The back legs appear first and then the front legs.

3. The tadpoles hatch out of the eggs. They have long tails for swimming, gills for breathing and no legs. They eat water plants at first but as they grow older they also eat small invertebrates.

Mandy Brockbank

The lifecycle of reptiles

Reptiles have a far simpler lifecycle than frogs. Baby reptiles are born smaller versions of their parents – much like humans. They don't go through metamorphosis.

The **water monitor** hatchling is a smaller version of its parents.

Most reptiles leave their eggs once they are laid and the young have to fend for themselves. Others, like crocodiles and some lizards and snakes, guard their eggs until they hatch. When a parent looks after its eggs and young, this is called 'parental care'.

Where do reptiles lay their eggs?

Reptiles always lay their eggs on land, even crocodiles and terrapins, which spend so much time in the water.

Most reptile eggs are surrounded by soft, leathery skin. They are usually buried to protect them from drying out in the sun. Some reptiles, like geckos, do not bury their eggs. They lay hard-shelled eggs, like birds' eggs.

Atherton de Villiers

Common egg-eaters hatch from eggs. Learn more about egg-eaters on page 189.

Most reptiles are oviparous. This means they lay eggs, like birds do. But some reptiles don't lay eggs. The babies develop inside the mother's body and are born live. These animals are viviparous. Examples of viviparous reptiles are dwarf chameleons (on page 177) and some skinks, snakes and lizards.

Conservation matters

Conservation came about because so many animals and plants were disappearing from the earth. Conservation is a way of looking after the natural world.

What are the problems?

1. Frogs and reptiles are losing their habitat! There are so many people that there are fewer and fewer places left for animals to live.

2. Humans use chemical poisons in gardening and farming. Rivers and other wetlands are polluted with toxic waste from industries. Frogs absorb these pollutants straight through their skin.

3. Alien plants invade the natural habitat and replace indigenous vegetation.

5. Many species of reptile, including crocodiles, monitor lizards and turtles, are hunted for their skins and shells to make shoes, belts, bags, wallets and other fashion items. Frogs are also hunted for food.

4. Many reptiles, such as pythons (see page 187), are popular pets. They are often taken out of the wild to keep as pets or sold in the pet trade.

Atherton de Villiers

A road was built through this wetland habitat, where the critically endangered micro frog lived. Learn about the micro frog on page 162.

An endangered frog

The **Table Mountain ghost frog** is critically endangered. This means it faces an extremely high risk of extinction in the wild. It is only found in a few streams on Table Mountain in Cape Town. Alien plants, visitors to Table Mountain and too many veld fires are changing its natural habitat.

Atherton de Villiers

The Table Mountain ghost frog

How can you help?

- Create natural habitats in your garden. For example, plant an indigenous garden or create a rockery, pond or wetland.
- Don't use chemical poisons in the garden. Rather use organic products where you can.
- If you think that an environment or wetland is being polluted or destroyed illegally, report it to the environmental officer at your local municipality.
- Only buy healthy animals from trustworthy pet shops and breeders. Never buy animals that may have been caught from the wild or illegally brought into the country. It is against the law to keep an indigenous animal as a pet without a permit.
- Get rid of alien plants in your garden or neighborhood. Get your school or community involved.

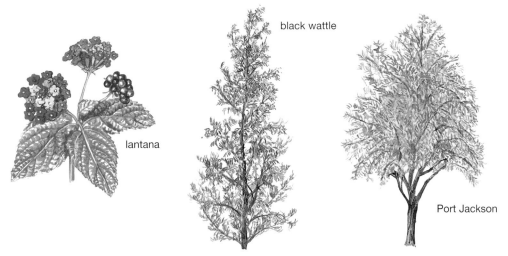

black wattle

lantana

Port Jackson

Here are some examples of alien plants that spread easily and take over the indigenous habitat. You can help by taking them out of your garden.

The world's most threatened tortoise

The **geometric tortoise** is considered the world's most threatened tortoise. It lives in a small area in the south-western Cape. Only 3% of its habitat is left because humans have developed the land for farming and housing. The first tortoise reserve in Africa was proclaimed in 1972 to protect this tortoise.

The geometric tortoise

Atherton de Villiers

▶ Frogs

Why are frogs different?

Frogs have naked skin. They don't have hair like mammals, feathers like birds or scales like reptiles. Their skin is also permeable. This means that substances like water and oxygen can pass freely through tiny pores on the surface of their skin.

Frogs can actually breathe through their skin (see opposite). For a frog to survive, its skin must be kept moist. It secretes mucus (a thin, slimy substance) to cover and protect the skin. Frogs moult about once a week to once a month to keep their skin thin and permeable.

Frogs lose water through their skin

Frogs are usually found close to water. This is because when it is dry, they dry out by losing all their body water through their permeable skin. If they don't live close to water, they hide underground, like toads and rainfrogs do (see pages 156 and 159).

Frogs are mostly active at night, because the air is cool and moist.

Frogs are excellent **bio-indicators**. A bio-indicator is a living creature that tells us something about the environment it lives in. The more frogs there are in an area, the healthier the environment is. This is because frogs are very sensitive to water or air pollution because pollutants pass easily through their skin.

How do frogs breathe?

Lungs: Have you ever watched a frog and noticed that its throat moves up and down all the time? This is how it breathes. Frogs use their throats to pump air in and out of their lungs via their nostrils. Humans breathe by expanding and relaxing their chests to get air in and out of their lungs.

Read about this **guttural toad** on page 156.

Skin: Frogs also use their skin to breathe. A frog's skin is thin and covered in a thin, slimy substance called mucus. There are many blood vessels just under the surface of a frog's skin. When oxygen in the air comes into contact with the skin, it dissolves in the mucus. Then it passes into the blood vessels because a frog's skin is permeable.

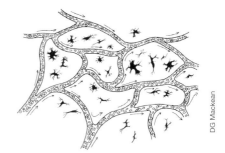

There is a network of blood vessels under a frog's skin.

Gills: Tadpoles live in water. They don't have lungs. They breathe using their gills. The gills are packed with tiny blood vessels that absorb oxygen from the water. As tadpoles turn into frogs, they lose their gills and grow lungs.

A **raucous toad** tadpole

Frogs don't drink water. They get the water they need by absorbing it through their skin.

Platannas

Platannas or platies, like the **common platanna**, spend their whole lives under the water.

They are smooth and slippery so they can glide through the water. This also helps them slip away from their enemies, such as waterbirds. They have strong back legs, large feet and webbed toes, which are adapted for swimming.

Jelger Herder

Platannas will leave the water to find another pond if their pond dries up. They will also bury themselves under the mud until rain comes.

Catching food

Platannas are totally different to all other frogs and toads because they don't have a tongue. They don't need one because they swallow their prey whole under the water. They use their front feet to push it into their mouths. If the prey is very large, they tear it apart with the claws on their back feet.

Common platanna tadpoles eat loads of mosquito larvae and other water insects. They in turn are eaten by water beetles and dragonfly larvae.

Common platanna (clawed toad)
Xenopus laevis (5–10 cm)
Like snakes, platannas don't have any eyelids so they can't shut their eyes. But they don't need to because their eyes are kept moist under the water, like fish eyes.

River frogs

River frogs, for example **common** and **Cape river frogs**, always live next to permanent water, like rivers, dams or garden ponds.

They have smooth belly skin and long, pointed noses, which make them very streamlined. They also have very long toes for grasping onto reeds and rocks. Their toes are strongly webbed for swimming.

Kevin Drummond-Hay

River frogs are streamlined, which helps them move through the water easily.

Common river frog
Amietia angolensis (4–9 cm)
River frogs have very long, powerful legs for jumping and swimming. They can jump up to 5 metres.

How can frogs stay under the water for so long?

River frogs usually sit at the water's edge but 'plop' into water if there is danger nearby. They can hide at the bottom of the water for as long as 45 minutes. How do they stay under water for so long? Frogs can absorb oxygen from the water through the tiny pores on the surface of their skin. Read more about this on page 153.

Cape river frog
Amietia fuscigula (7.5–12 cm)

tympanum (see below)

What is a tympanum?

Tympanums are a frog's ears. They are thin layers of skin stretched tightly, like small circles, just behind the eyes. They protect the opening into the ear. Frogs can hear in the air and under water.

Toads

Toads, like **guttural**, **raucous** or **western leopard toads**, live mostly on land, often far from water.

They are very common in gardens. They have short back legs used for walking or making small hops, and they have dry, rough, warty skin. The warty, horny skin is protection against drying out because they live far from water. Learn about frog skin on pages 152–153.

Guttural toad
Amietophrynus gutturalis
(5–7.5 cm)

Raucous toad
Amietophrynus rangeri
(up to 10 cm)

They still need water for breeding

During the day, toads burrow under the ground to protect themselves from the sun. They come out at night to feed on insects.

Although they live on land, they still need to lay their eggs in water. In the mating season, they gather together at pools and marshes to mate and lay their eggs.

Raucous toads call very loudly to the females *'kwaak, kwaak'*, which means 'come and mate with me'.

'Don't touch that toad, you'll get warts!'

It is definitely not true when someone says this to you! It's a myth.

Toads have poison glands, called paratoid glands, behind their eyes. These produce a white, liquid poison that looks like milk. The 'milk' covers the body and protects them from predators. This liquid is horrible to taste. Most cats and dogs avoid toads.

paratoid gland

Western leopard toad
Amietophrynus patherinus (7.5 cm)
This toad has lost so much of its habitat to human development that it is now an endangered species.

Sand frogs

Sand frogs are like toads because they have a similar body shape and warty skin. They spend some time on land away from water so their legs are short and they have blunt noses. Compare them with the river frog's pointed nose on page 155. Sand frogs move in short jumps. In the rainy season, they get together to mate and lay eggs in shallow waters of pools, marshes and dams.

Different places, different frogs

Knowing where frogs live and what habitat they prefer helps to identify them. The **Natal sand frog** is found all over KwaZulu-Natal. It prefers open or bushy habitat. The **Cape sand frog** is found along the Cape coast. It prefers open sand and grassland habitats. Learn more about this on page 138.

Cape sand frog
Tomopterna delalandii
(5 cm)

Natal sand frog
Tomopterna natalensis
(4.5 cm)

What do their feet tell us?

Sand frogs and toads have short toes with very little webbing. These are adaptations for life on land. They have small, hard ridges or bumps, called tubercles, on the heel of each back foot. They use these for digging holes into the ground backwards. They hide in these holes in the day and 'hibernate' in them during the dry months of the year. Read about hibernating on page 141.

tubercle

Louis du Preez

A tubercle is used for digging.

The feet and toes of frogs are one of the ways we identify them. Have a look at the toes of all the frogs in this section of the book. Can you guess why they need these adaptations?

Chirping and moss frogs

Chirping and moss frogs don't lay their eggs in water and the tadpoles never swim. Instead, they lay their eggs in a nest, which they make in a damp hole in the ground, hidden by rocks or vegetation.

The tadpoles wriggle around on the wet ground and feed off the egg yolk while they quickly go through metamorphosis and become baby frogs. Learn about the frog lifecycle on page 148.

Where do they live?

Chirping and moss frogs don't spend much time in water. For this reason they have no webbing between their toes. But they are both always found in damp or wet places, like where water seeps or oozes out of the ground, or near streams or waterfalls in forests. They use vegetation, leaf litter, or muddy or rocky holes for shelter and protection from predators.

Different places, different frogs

Cape Peninsula moss frog
Arthroleptella lightfooti (2 cm)
Moss frogs are only found in the Western Cape.
This one is only found on the Cape Peninsula.
It has lost a great deal of its habitat to humans
and is a threatened species.

Natal chirping frog
Anhydrophryne hewitti (3 cm)
Chirping frogs are only found in the Eastern
Cape and KwaZulu-Natal. This one is only
found in the Drakensberg and Midlands of
KwaZulu-Natal.

Look deep into my eyes...

Look at the shapes of frogs' pupils in this section. Herpetologists use frog pupils to help identify different species.

The pupils of chirping, moss and bullfrogs are egg-shaped and lie horizontally. Tree frogs have egg-shaped pupils but they lie vertically. Have a look on page 146. Platanna pupils are round, like human ones. See page 154.

Rain frogs

Rain frogs, like **plain** and **Mozambique rain frogs**, are strange-looking frogs. They have big, sack-like bodies with flat faces and small legs and arms. As you can imagine, rain frogs can't jump or swim. They only walk or waddle. They are called 'rain frogs' because they only appear for three months after the first rains to mate. Otherwise, they live in holes underground, where they 'hibernate'. For this reason rain frogs can live in many different kinds of habitats, from forest to desert. Read about hibernation on page 141.

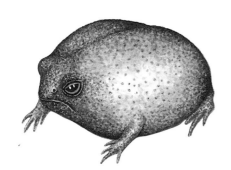
Plain rain frog
Breviceps fuscus (5 cm)

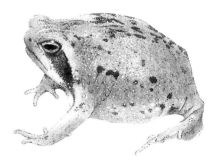
Mozambique rain frog
Breviceps mossambicus (5 cm)

Nests built underground

Rain frogs lay their eggs in a chamber underground that the female digs with her back feet. The female covers her eggs with extra jelly after the eggs are laid to keep them moist. The tadpoles develop inside the jelly and then hatch as perfectly formed baby frogs.

Escaping predators

The Afrikaans name '*blaasop*', meaning 'blow up', describes rain frogs very well. When disturbed, they blow themselves up into a hard ball and then let out a breath with a '*hiss*' and a '*miaow*'. This is to make themselves look bigger and scare off predators.

Rain frogs have a hard ridge, called a tubercle, on the heel of each back foot, which acts like a spade for digging. They use it to dig backwards into the ground. Have a look at what a tubercle looks like on page 157.

Climbing frogs

Reed frogs

Reed frogs are great climbers. They have sticky pads or discs at the end of each toe. This helps them to stick to reeds and other plants they like climbing. They call at night from water plants in marshes and pools. In the day, they are often found far from water, where they shelter in trees and the leaves of other plants. Have a look at the **painted reed frog** in the photograph.

Jelger Herder

A **painted reed frog** can sit for hours with its legs tucked in while warming itself in the sun's rays.

Confusing predators

Reed frogs have a clever way of escaping predators. When they jump, the inside of their legs flash orange-pink, but as soon as they land, the colour disappears. This makes them seem to disappear too!

Painted reed frog *Hyperolius marmoratus* (2.5–3.5 cm)
The colours and patterns of the painted reed frog change depending on where you find them.

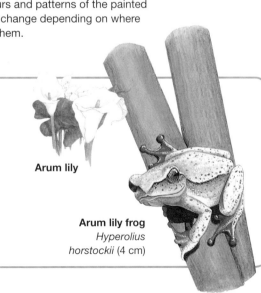

Arum lily

Using camouflage

Arum lily frogs often hide in arum lily flowers and ambush insects visiting to feed on the flower. They camouflage themselves by changing their colour to closely match the colour of the flower. They have orange-pink coloured legs and toes, which they tuck into their bodies to help with the disguise.

Arum lily frog *Hyperolius horstockii* (4 cm)

Leaf-folding frogs

Greater leaf-folding frogs have sticky pads on their toes for climbing. They climb up reeds or other water plants to make their nests above the water.

They actually fold and glue the edges of a leaf together with sticky fluids they make. The eggs are hidden inside the leaf. They are protected from predators and from drying out in the sun. When the tadpoles hatch, the glue softens and they fall into the water below.

Greater leaf-folding frog *Afrixalus fornasinii* (3 cm)

Foam nest frogs

Foam nest frogs climb into trees hanging over water to nest. They also have suckers or sticky pads on their toes for climbing, like reed and leaf-folding frogs.

The female grey tree frog produces a fluid that she beats into foam using her back legs. The eggs are laid in the foam and mixed in. The outside of the nest dries in the sun, forming a hard crust. It protects the eggs from predators and also stops them from drying out in the sun. After hatching, the tadpoles break through the crust and fall into the water below.

Foam nest frog *Chiromantis xerampelina* (4 cm)
The white foamy nests of the foam nest frog are often spotted hanging from branches or rocks above pans.

Dainty frogs

Boettger's cacos are very small, dainty frogs that hide most of the year. After good rains, thousands of them appear to breed. They prefer shallow places that become flooded after the rain, like marshes and small rain pools. But they are hardly ever seen because they are so small and they hide among tufts of grass in the day.

Boettger's caco
Cacosternum boettgeri (2–2.5 cm)
Boettger's cacos can vary in colour from greys and browns to brilliant green, like in the photograph below.

Marius Burger

Male cacos call '*tick, tick, tick*' or '*terrik, terrrriiick*' loudly to the females in the mating season. The vocal sac gets to nearly half the size of the frog! Read about how frogs find a mate on page 146.

An endangered micro frog

The **micro frog** is the smallest frog in southern Africa. It is only 1.2–1.8 centimetres long. It is also a critically endangered species, which means it may go extinct very soon if it is not protected. Human development has destroyed its home and polluted the wetland habitat it needs to survive. Have a look at this on page 150. Alien plants have also taken over its habitat.

Atherton de Villiers

Micro frog *Microbatrachella capensis* (1.2–1.8 cm)

Bullfrogs

The biggest frog in southern Africa

The **giant bullfrog** is the biggest frog in southern Africa. It can weigh more than a kilogram! It eats almost any animals, including birds, rats, reptiles, toads, crabs, snails and insects. It has small bony 'teeth' on its bottom jaw for holding onto its prey so it can't escape. It protects itself by blowing itself up and snapping with wide jaws. It can bite!

Giant bullfrog
Pyxicephalus adspersus
(11–24 cm)

They hide for most of the year

Bullfrogs spend most of the year buried underground. Learn about hibernation on page 141. They have a hard ridge on the heel of each back foot, called a tubercle, for digging (see page 157). They bury themselves in a cocoon made from their own skin. After heavy summer rains, rain pools or pans form for a short time. Bullfrogs come out of the ground to use these shallow pools for breeding.

Louis du Preez

A male bullfrog calls in his habitat. He calls to the females to come and mate with him. His call sounds like a cow mooing loudly inside a tunnel!

Giant bullfrogs are under threat because their grassland and wetland habitats are being taken over by human development. Read more about conservation matters on page 150.

▶ Reptiles

What are reptiles?

'Reptile' means 'creeping' or 'crawling', which is exactly what reptiles do. But many can also swim, run and glide through the air. Reptiles are very different from frogs. They have dry, scaly skin and don't need moisture or water to survive, like frogs do. Their skin is made up of small, hard plates called scales. The scales make a waterproof layer to stop water being lost from the body. Reptiles can live in hot, desert-like places, where most frogs would not survive.

Tessa Oliver

Read more about rock monitors like this one on page 181.

Getting rid of old skin

The thicker outside layer of a reptile's skin is shed as it gets old and worn down and a new layer forms. This is called moulting. Moulting also gets rid of skin parasites and allows the animal to grow bigger. The animal moults one to four times a year.

David Maguire

Snakes shed their entire skin at one time, including the scales that cover their eyes.

Kirsty Kyle

Most lizards, like this chameleon, shed their skin in large flakes.

Tortoises and terrapins

Reptiles with a shell

Tortoises, terrapins and turtles are the only reptiles with a shell. As a group they are called **chelonians**. They are also the only animals that have a shell on the outside of their bodies as well as a skeleton on the inside. The shell is actually joined to the tortoise's backbone and ribs.

A chelonian's shell is made of bone. It can be covered with large, horny scales, like we see in tortoises, or leathery skin, like leatherback turtles. Chelonians don't have teeth. They have sharp, horny jaws, like a bird's beak, which they use for cutting up or chewing through their food.

Tortoises live on land.

Terrapins live in freshwater.

Turtles live in the sea. We have not included any turtles in this book.

Leatherback turtle
Dermochelys coriacea (2.8 m)

165

Tortoises live on land

Land tortoises, like **leopard** and **angulate tortoises**, have thick, dome-shaped shells. They have thick legs for carrying their heavy shells around.

They are herbivores, which means they eat plants, such as grasses, herbs, flowers and fruit. They also eat bones and hyena faeces, which give them calcium for strengthening their shells and eggshells.

Spot the difference

Leopard tortoise *Stigmochelys pardalis*
(30–45 cm, up to 70 cm)
The leopard tortoise is the largest and most widely spread tortoise in southern Africa. It's named after the dark spots on its shell.

Angulate tortoise *Chersina angulata*
(15–25 cm)
The angulate tortoise only lives in sandy areas of the Cape in South Africa. It has bold grey to black markings.

Claws for digging

Tortoises have long claws for digging. They dig holes to lay their eggs in or for 'hibernating' during the winter (see page 141). After hatching, young tortoises dig their way to the surface.

The eggs have soft shells and are easy prey for many animals, such as birds of prey, hyenas, jackals, mongooses, dogs and monitor lizards.

Southern Africa has the greatest diversity of tortoises in the world! We have 14 different species. Many tortoises are taken from the wild or found on the road. They suffer or die because they can't survive out of their natural habitat or are not looked after properly. Read more about conservation matters on page 150.

Speed verses body armour

Tortoises definitely can't rely on speed to escape predators! They use their shells for protection. They hide inside their shells when there is danger about.

The shell also protects them from the sun so tortoises can live in very dry places.

For protection, tortoises pull their heads inside their shells. Then they pull in their heavily scaled front legs, so the head is hidden behind them.

Jelger Herder

The winner gets his mate

Tortoises live by themselves. They only pair up in spring and early summer to mate. If two males of the same kind meet during this period, they often end up fighting. They shove and butt each other, testing out each other's strength.

The strongest male gets to mate with the female. He follows the female around until she mates with him. He even butts and shoves her to let her know he won't give up!

Wessel Badenhorst

Angulate tortoises mate in spring and summer.

Tortoises help plants by spreading their seeds. Tortoises don't chew their food and the seeds pass through the gut without getting damaged.

Hinged tortoises

Hinged tortoises have a special hinge at the back of their shells. They close the hinge after pulling the back legs and tail inside the shell for protection. They are a little different from other tortoises because they also eat meat, such as millipedes, beetles and snails.

The **Natal hinged tortoise** is endemic to South Africa. This means it is not found anywhere else. It only lives in a small part of KwaZulu-Natal and Mpumalanga.

Natal hinged tortoise
Kinixys natalensis
(8–12 cm)

Padlopers

Padlopers are small tortoises with flatter shells than other tortoises. They are endemic to southern Africa, which means they are not found anywhere else. They are mostly found in the Cape in South Africa, often on rocky ground. If they fall over onto their backs, they are able to right themselves.

The **speckled padloper** is the world's smallest tortoise. The shell is about 6–8 cm long.

Atherton de Villiers

This **parrot-beaked** or **common padloper** has a hooked beak. The shell is about 7–9 cm.

Carol Broomhall

The speckled padloper is threatened because it has lost so much of its habitat to farming. It is also illegally collected for the pet trade. The parrot-beaked padloper and Natal hinged tortoise have similar problems.

Terrapins live in freshwater

The **marsh** and **serrated hinged terrapins** live in freshwater. They have light, flat shells and webbed back feet for pushing themselves through the water. They have strong claws on their feet for shredding their food and digging holes to 'hibernate' in when the water dries up or to bury their eggs. They are well camouflaged with their brown, grey or green shells, which helps with hunting prey and hiding from predators.

Deon Guyt

Marsh terrapins prefer muddy pans and marshes. They bask with their necks stretched out on rocks, logs or the water's edge.

Finding food

Marsh and hinged terrapins are omnivores. They eat water plants and animals, like insects, fish, tadpoles, frogs, crabs and birds. When hunting, they sneak up on their prey with just their heads or nostrils sticking out the water, or they hide right under the water. The nostrils are at the very tip of the snout. They have two or three short, soft tentacles under their chin. These help them feel where they are under the water.

Sally van der Woude

Serrated hinged terrapins prefer deeper open water. They often bask on floating logs and rocks to warm up in the sun. Sometimes they even bask on hippos' heads! They will pick the ticks off the skin of buffalo and hippos wallowing in the water. They also try to take a share of a crocodile's meal, but can sometimes become food for the crocodile!

The turtles shown in this section are part of a group of terrapins called the side-necked terrapins. They fold their heads in sideways under the shell so that just the side of their face and one eye can be seen. Tortoises pull their heads straight back into the shell. Their necks can bend into a tight S-shape!

Spot the difference

- **Marsh terrapins** are found all over southern Africa, even in desert-like places. They prefer to live in slow-moving or standing water, like muddy pans and marshes.
- Marsh terrapin shells are much flatter than those of hinged terrapins. There are no hinges at the front of the shell to cover the terrapins' head and front legs.
- To escape predators, marsh terrapins stir up the mud to hide. Their flat, muddy-coloured shells help with this camouflage. They also produce a disgusting-smelling liquid from stink glands. This smell can last for days.

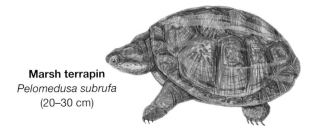

Marsh terrapin
Pelomedusa subrufa
(20–30 cm)

- **Serrated hinged terrapins** are mostly found in the north-eastern parts of southern Africa. They prefer to live in the deep, open water of large rivers, lakes and pans, which don't dry up.
- Hinged terrapins have a more rounded shell than marsh terrapins.
- They have a large hinge at the front of the shell. The hinge closes when the terrapin pulls its head into its shell. This protects the head and front legs from predators.

Serrated hinged terrapin
Pulusios sinuatus
(30–45 cm)

It helps to know what habitat an animal prefers to live in. This makes it easier to identify it and understand some of its behaviour. Read on pages 138–139 about the kinds of habitats we find in southern Africa.

The lizard group

This group includes the lizards, skinks, chameleons, geckos, agamas, leguaans or monitors and crocodiles. It is by far the largest group of reptiles. There are about 517 species in southern Africa. They have four legs, although some skinks have very small legs or no legs at all (see page 172).

A **tropical girdled lizard**. Read about these lizards on page 175.

Lizard senses

Lizards hunt using their eyes and ears. They hunt by ambushing their prey, which means they catch them by surprise. Unlike snakes, lizards have movable eyelids and ear holes on the sides of their heads. Eyelids are used for protecting their eyes. Some lizards, like geckos, don't have eyelids. They clean their eyes with their tongues. Some lizards, like the monitor lizard, use their forked tongues to smell, like snakes do. Read how snakes do this on page 185.

Van Son's geckos live on rocks. They hunt small insects at night using their large eyes. Their tails swell up when there is plenty of food around and act as fat-storage sites.

Skinks: unusual lizards

There is a great variety of skinks in southern Africa – 74 species have been described. They are different from lizards because they have a very short head and no obvious neck. They have very smooth, flat, polished scales, like most snakes. Compare them with the lizards on page 171.

Brigit Erni

This **Cape skink** is using the sun to warm itself up.

Skinks are mostly active in the day, when they hunt a wide variety of invertebrates, such as ants, termites, crickets, grasshoppers, beetles, flies, spiders and earthworms. Some live on the ground, others live on rocks and others live under the ground.

Burrowing skinks

Many skinks, like the dwarf and burrowing skinks, don't have any legs or have very small legs and long bodies. They have adapted to a life of burrowing through soil or leaf litter. These skinks can be confused with snakes. They are often killed because people think they are snakes. They will writhe or wriggle furiously to frighten-off predators, which also makes them look just like snakes!

Adele Pretorius

Short-legged dwarf burrowing skinks have long, thin bodies and very small legs.

Loot Ekstein

Legless skinks have no legs and a large beak-shaped scale over their snouts. Their eyes are also very different to snake eyes (see page 184). Skinks have movable eyelids, unlike snakes, which have no eyelids.

You can tell legless skinks from snakes by their belly scales. Snakes have very large scales on their bellies, while legless lizards have very small scales.

Camouflage

Most skinks have dull colours on their skin, which helps to camouflage them against predators. They are prey to many predators, such as jackals, birds and domestic cats. Many lizards, like skinks, have stripes that are used to confuse predators when they are moving.

Many lizards, like this **rainbow skink**, have bright blue tails. Herpetologists think this tail is used to attract the attention of predators. When the predator goes for the tail, they lose their tail to the predator instead of losing their lives.

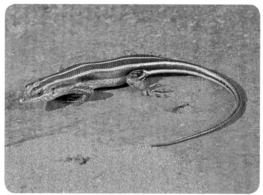

Jelger Herder

Spot the difference

Eastern striped skinks have thick, stripy bodies. They live mostly above the ground, such as on rocks, trees and the walls of houses. They have spiny scales under their feet and long, clawed toes, which help with climbing. They quickly run for cover when there is danger nearby. They hide in cracks or under rocks and logs.

Eastern striped skink
Trachylepis striata
(18–20 cm)

Cape skinks look like they eat too much because of their fat bodies! They live on the ground where they dig burrows into the sand under rocks, bushes or logs. This is where they take shelter or hide from predators.

Cape skink *Trachylepis capensis*
(20–25 cm)

Some reptiles, like skinks and geckos, can snap off their tails, which then wriggle around to distract a predator. Their tails grow back again in time. Other reptiles, like monitor lizards, chameleons, agamas and crocodiles, can't lose their tails. They have other ways of escaping predators.

Lizards that like crevices

The lizards shown on these pages live in rock cracks or crevices, which they use for shelter, protection and breeding. They will leave these crevices to hunt but always dash back to safety if there is danger about.

Marius Burger

Cape crag lizard

Outsmarting predators

The **Cape crag lizard** sticks its head into a rock crack and then clenches its jaws so that its head gets thicker and jams inside the crack. Most of these lizards have head shields made of thick bony plates for protecting their heads when they jam themselves into these cracks.

Some lizards, like the **giant plated lizard**, avoid being eaten by hiding in rock cracks and then blowing their bodies up. It's very difficult to get them out as they get firmly stuck.

Giant lizards

The **giant plated lizard** is a huge lizard. It prefers to live on large rocky outcrops. Its body is covered in small, thick scales that look like rows of neat squares. The scales are used for protection on rough rocks and from predators.

Giant plated lizard
Gerrhosaurus validus
(40–60 cm)

The giant plated lizard is a protected species because it is a popular reptile to keep as a pet here and overseas. Too many are taken out of the wild! Learn more about conservation matters on page 150.

Body armour

Girdled lizards have body armour to protect them from predators. The body armour is made from hard, bony plates under the scales. The bony scales go right round the whole body. The tail and sometimes the head are also covered in spiny scales.

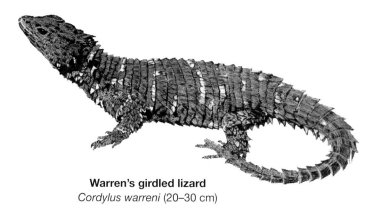

Warren's girdled lizard
Cordylus warreni (20–30 cm)

Girdled lizards live in colonies where there are good rock cracks. Within these colonies, the bigger, stronger males hold the best territories. The males compete for territories by bobbing their heads at each other. They size each other up in this way, trying to figure out who is the fittest and strongest. If one is not scared off, they will fight. The winner has a better chance of finding a mate.

Crag lizards

The **Drakensberg crag lizard** prefers mountainous areas, where it finds an open rock crack to live in. The males are very territorial over a rock crack and fight with other males to keep them off.

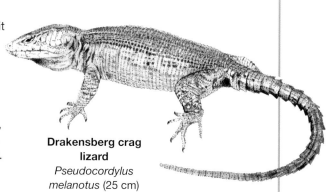

Drakensberg crag lizard
Pseudocordylus melanotus (25 cm)

In the breeding season, the males display bright colours of red, black, orange or yellow to attract females and warn other males to stay away. The females are dark brown, to blend in with the background.

Extraordinary lizards

Chameleons are extraordinary lizards! They have adapted to a life of climbing. They have a special prehensile tail. 'Prehensile' means 'gripping' because the tail grips like a finger by curling around a branch. Their feet act like pincers and are also used for gripping tightly to branches.

Masters of camouflage

Chameleons use camouflage and very slow movement to escape being seen by predators. They can change the colour of their skin to match their surroundings. They also hunt for prey in this way. They use their long, sticky tongues to catch prey. Have a look at this on page 143.

Flap-necked chameleon

Independent eyes

A chameleon's eyes can move independently, which means one eye can move forwards while the other moves backwards. They can keep an eye out for prey and predators in front and behind them at the same time!

At night, the **flap-neck chameleon** turns bright blue-white to blend in with the night. During the day it blends in with the vegetation by turning different shades of green, yellow and brown, and adding or losing dark spots.

This flap-neck blends in so well between the grass blades that you can hardly see it!

Dwarf chameleons

Dwarf chameleons are very small chameleons. They have spiny crests along their backs and throats, which they blow up when they feel threatened.

They are different from the larger chameleons in that they give birth to live young rather than lay eggs. They are endemic to southern Africa. 'Endemic' means they are only found here and nowhere else.

Cape dwarf chameleon
Bradypodion pumilum (12–16 cm)

Marienne de Villiers

Attracting a mate

Male dwarf chameleons become more colourful in the breeding season. They use their colours to challenge other males and attract a female.

The females and young are brown and grey-green for camouflage.

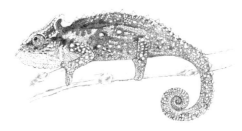

Natal Midlands dwarf chameleon
Bradypodion thamnobates (15–18 cm)

Fighting for a mate

All chameleons have a helmet behind their heads. This is called a casque, which is like a bony outgrowth. The males have a larger casque than the females. The males use them for head-butting each other when they fight for territories.

Drakensberg dwarf chameleon
Bradypodion dracomontanum (13–16 cm)

Dwarf chameleons often live in small, localised colonies. 'Localised' means they are only found in a particular area or region. Read the names of the chameleons shown on this page and see where each one is found.

Geckos

Geckos make up the biggest group of lizards. There are 111 species of geckos in southern Africa. Some examples are ground geckos, tree geckos, web-footed geckos, leaf-toed geckos, flat geckos and barking geckos.

Gecko's eyes don't have eyelids but are covered in a transparent skin. This means they never blink and they clean their eyes with their tongues. Geckos are mostly nocturnal, which means they are active at night. Nocturnal geckos have very large eyes for seeing in the dark.

Camouflage colours

Geckos have excellent camouflage. They blend in with the dull grey-brown colours and patterns on their skin. They can lighten or darken their colour to blend in better. In this way they can sneak up on their prey or escape being seen by predators.

Moreau's tropical house gecko

Special clinging toes

Most geckos live above the ground. Their feet are adapted for climbing. They can climb straight up walls or even upside down on ceilings! The tips of their toes are spread out and covered in special scales or tiny ridges. The ridges are covered in millions of tiny hairs, which allow them to cling to any surface.

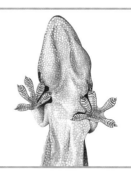

Geckos are the only lizards that can talk to each other! The male gecko clicks its tongue against the roof of its mouth, 'tik-tik-tik'. It lets other geckos know where he and his territory are. If intruders do not stay away, he will bite them to defend his spot.

Geckos in our homes

Many geckos live inside and around our homes because they are ideal places to live! The geckos shown on this page are examples. Our houses offer shelter from bad weather and protection from predators. They also provide ample food. This is because most geckos hunt at night and our lights attract many insects, which is what geckos mostly eat.

The geckos shown here are often spotted hunting on the walls and ceilings of our homes at night. They all have special clinging toes for climbing, like those shown on the opposite page. These geckos actually benefit us because they eat mosquitoes, flies and cockroaches that are often pests in our homes.

Spot the difference

Marbled African leaf-toed gecko
Afrogecko porphyreus (8–9 cm)
This gecko naturally lives in trees or on rocky outcrops. In the day it shelters under bark or in cracks and crevices.

Moreau's tropical house gecko
Hemidactylus mabouia (12–16 cm)
This gecko is very common in and around buildings and homes. Because geckos can change colour for camouflage, this gecko looks very pale and almost transparent when hunting under our night lights. Its natural habitat is in trees and under tree bark.

Dwarf geckos

This small gecko hunts termites and ants in the day. At night it takes shelter under peeling bark, in hollow stems or rock cracks. It has also adapted to hunting small insects around our homes at night.

Cape dwarf gecko
Lygodactylus capensis (6–7 cm)

Use the reference books listed at the back of this book on page 265 to find out more about these geckos. You should be able to find many of them at your local library.

Agamas

Agamas have large, triangular-shaped heads with large, bulging eyes and an obvious neck you don't see on other lizards. They have sharp front teeth used for cutting up and chewing their prey. They prefer to eat ants and termites, but will also eat beetles and other insects.

Male agamas develop bright colours in the breeding season to warn-off other males and attract a female. Read how they win a mate on page 147. The females and young have camouflage colours to hide from predators.

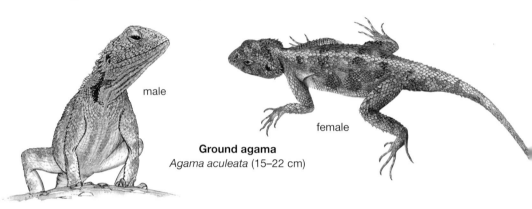

male

female

Ground agama
Agama aculeata (15–22 cm)

Favourite places to live

Agamas have favourite places to live. **Southern tree agamas** live in trees, often in gardens. **Ground agamas** live on the ground. Then there are agamas that prefer to live on rocks. They all find holes to sleep in at night. Read more about habitat preferences of different animals on page 138.

Southern tree agama
Acanthocercus atricollis (20–35 cm)
A breeding male has a bright blue head and upper body.

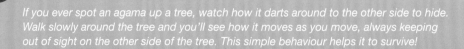

If you ever spot an agama up a tree, watch how it darts around to the other side to hide. Walk slowly around the tree and you'll see how it moves as you move, always keeping out of sight on the other side of the tree. This simple behaviour helps it to survive!

The largest lizards

Monitor lizards or leguaans are among the largest lizards in the world! They have large, strong legs and feet with long claws for digging holes into the ground, climbing and finding food. They use these holes for resting, 'hibernating' in winter or laying their eggs.

Monitor lizards smell using their forked tongues, like snakes do. Read how on page 185.

Who are their enemies?

Crocodiles, pythons, large eagles and honey badgers are leguaans' main enemies. They protect themselves by lashing out with their powerful tails and biting. If this does not work, they will quickly scurry away or play dead, sometimes for hours!

Rudi Jeggle

Spot the difference

Rock monitor
Varanus albigularis
(0.7–1.1 m)

Water monitor
Varanus niloticus
(1–1.4 m)

The **rock monitor** lives in savanna and semi-desert areas. It feeds on invertebrates, tortoises, eggs, small birds, rodents and even carrion. The **water monitor** is a good swimmer. It lives close to rivers and dams and hunts fish, crabs, frogs, snakes and snails.

Crocodiles

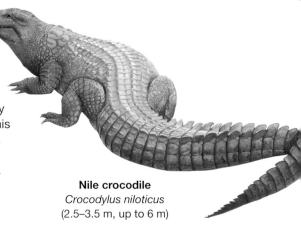

There is only one crocodile

The **Nile crocodile** is the only species of crocodile in southern Africa. It is very well adapted for swimming in water. This is where it hunts for food. It has a long, thick tail for pushing itself through the water. It uses its back legs for steering. It has webbed feet to help with fast turns and sudden movements.

Nile crocodile
Crocodylus niloticus
(2.5–3.5 m, up to 6 m)

Conservation matters

Crocodiles are actually threatened in the wild. Their habitat has been changed by humans and they can only really do well inside large reserves where they are not dangerous to humans.

Crocodile hatchlings

Crocodile mothers are one of the few reptiles to look after their young. The young are tasty treats for large waterbirds and many other predators. She carries the hatchlings in her mouth from her nest in a sandbank to a nursery area she has prepared for them in the water. Even though she looks after her young, only about one out of 50 hatchlings will survive.

Jelger Herder

Crocodiles grow from tiny hatchlings into very big adults.

The temperature of the soil in which the eggs are incubated determines whether the young crocodiles will be male or female. If eggs develop at high temperatures, they will be male. If they develop at low temperatures, they will be female.

How do crocodiles hunt?

Crocodiles have long snouts and strong jaws with sharp teeth for catching prey. They eat fish, other reptiles and mammals. They also eat carrion and clean up around the water by eating any rotten meat left lying around.

1. Crocodiles hunt large prey, like zebra, by ambushing them when they come down to the water to drink. They hide under the water and are well camouflaged. Just their eyes, nose and ears stick out.

2. Their senses of smell and sight are good. When they are close enough, they rush out of the water, grabbing the animal's leg or nose.

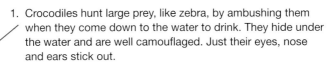

3. The crocodile drags the animal under the water to drown it. Other crocodiles will rush in to eat as much as possible.

4. Crocodiles tear their prey apart by clamping a part of it between their sharp, interlocking teeth. The teeth are not used for chewing, but for powerful gripping.

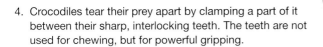

5. Crocodiles tear large prey apart by jerking their heads to and fro or rolling over and over in the water to break off pieces of meat. The pieces are then swallowed whole.

Crocodiles have 60 to 80 teeth. Each tooth is shed 2 to 3 times a year, so a crocodile sheds about 200 teeth a year!

Snakes

Slithering snakes

Snakes have long, slender bodies, covered in scaly skin. They don't have legs and move mostly from side to side in an S-shape. They would not be able to do this without a very flexible backbone. Snakes can have as many as 200 to 400 bones in their back and as many ribs along the length of their body (humans only have 24 ribs). The snake's ribs keep its shape and help with movement.

Can snakes hear and see?

Snakes don't have eyelids like other reptiles. Instead, they have a transparent scale over each eye to protect it. Because of this, most snakes can really only follow movement. Scales also cover their ear holes so they cannot hear sound in the air like humans can. They have other special ways of finding their prey. Read about this on the opposite page.

Malcolm Douglas

Olive grass snake

Special senses

Snakes capture and eat live animals. They use some extraordinary senses to find their prey.

Smelling with forked tongues

Most snakes use their forked tongues to smell. A snake flicks its tongue in and out of its mouth to pick up smells from the air or ground.

There are two openings in the roof of a snake's mouth, which lead to a sensitive spot called the Jacobson's organ. This organ sends a message to the brain telling it what it has smelt.

Marius Burger

Eastern tiger snake

Why is a snake's tongue forked?

Each side of the fork can pick up a different smell. If a snake is looking for prey, it can tell which direction the prey has moved. Monitor lizards also smell using forked tongues like snakes do. Read more about them on page 181.

Hearing through the skin

Snakes hear through their skin! Sound waves or vibrations from the air or ground hit the skin and are passed from the muscle under the skin to the bone.

Snakes don't have ears on the outside, like humans do. But they have ear bones on the inside. The vibrations reach the ear bones through the jawbones.

Myles Veysey

Namib sand snake

Snakes that are not venomous

All the snakes from this page to page 190 are non-venomous. Non-venomous snakes don't use poison to kill their prey. They eat prey whole or kill them first using constriction. Constriction is when the snake wraps its body around its prey and squeezes until the prey can't breathe and dies.

Most non-venomous snakes have many sharp, backward-pointing teeth, like short hooks. The teeth lock onto the prey so it can't escape.
A snake's teeth cannot chew so snakes always swallow their prey whole. See page 143 for how snakes are able swallow prey larger than themselves.

Nick Helme

A **spotted house snake** kills its prey by constriction. It is not venomous.

How do scales help?

Reptiles' bodies are covered with scales. The scales of snakes feel smooth and dry.

- Scales protect the body.
- Scales help with movement. The belly scales of snakes are large and thick and move easily across the ground. The scales grip while the muscles move the body forward.
- Scales stop moisture escaping from the body.
- Scales help with camouflage.

Marius Burger

Brown house snake

The largest snake in Africa

The **southern African python** is the largest snake in Africa. It is very powerful and can weigh over 40 kilograms. It eats rodents, dassies, birds, monkeys, baboons and buck up to the size of an impala. It hunts from a hidden position when the sun goes down. It attacks by ambushing its prey.

Pythons lay between 20 and 100 eggs the size of tennis balls in a large hollow, like inside an old termite mound. They are one of the few snakes that look after their eggs.

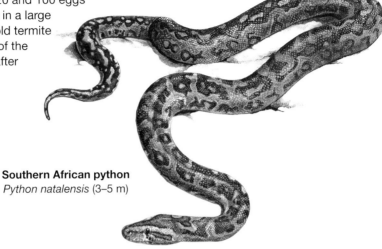

Southern African python
Python natalensis (3–5 m)

Special heat detectors

Some snakes, like pythons, have super-sensitive heat detectors that find warm-blooded prey by their body heat. The heat detectors are small holes called pits found on the front of the face or lips. They can pick up very tiny changes in temperature. These pits are useful for finding prey in the dark.

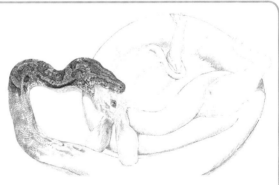

Pythons kill their prey by constriction.
Then they swallow it whole.

Pythons are protected because they are hunted for food and for their tough skin, which is used to make leather. They are also used in traditional medicine, and young pythons are popular in the pet trade. Read more about conservation matters on page 150.

Water snakes

Water snakes are nocturnal. They are called water snakes because they live in wet areas, such as dams, rivers or streams. They are excellent swimmers. They dive under the water to hide from predators or to catch prey. They mainly eat frogs and tadpoles, and sometimes fish. They kill their prey by constriction before swallowing them.

Common brown water snake
Lycodonomorphus rufulus (60–80 cm)
Frogs are a favourite food of this snake.

Water snakes are harmless to humans. They can become quite tame and gentle pets. They are protected in some areas because humans have destroyed their habitat. Read more about conservation matters on page 150.

House snakes

House snakes are often found around houses, which is where they get their name. They live on the ground and are nocturnal. They are harmless to humans and make great pets. They eat rats, mice, lizards, frogs and often other snakes. House snakes are prey to many animals, such as cobras, owls and genets.

Jelger Herder

Brown house snake
Lamprophis fuliginosus
(60–100 cm)

This is one of the better-known house snakes because it's found all over southern Africa.

Egg-eaters

An egg-eater, like the **common egg-eater**, only eats birds' eggs. It has some amazing adaptations for swallowing eggs, which are often much larger than its head!

How does it eat eggs?

- It has loose skin around the lower jaw and neck, which can stretch like elastic.
- The jawbones can come apart when the snake opens its mouths so the mouth becomes huge.
- Once the egg is swallowed, the snake uses its throat muscles to push the egg against the neck vertebrae. Bony teeth on the neck vertebrae cut into the egg to break it open.
- The egg-eater swallows the egg contents and then spits out the shell.

Common egg-eater
(rhombic egg-eater)
Dasypeltis scabra (50–90 cm)

Mole eaters

The **mole snake** is a large snake that hunts moles during the day. It kills them by constriction. It also eats rats and mice. Farmers consider it a friend because it actually helps to control the numbers of these animals.

Because of this, the mole snake was one of the first snakes to be protected by law. But humans often kill them because they attack and bite if they are scared.

Mole snake
Pseudaspis cana
(1–2 m)

Mole snakes are one of the few snake species in the world where the males fight seriously at mating time. They bite each other, leaving big holes. Other snakes prefer combat dancing. Read about this on page 147.

Slug-eaters

Slug-eaters are small snakes that eat slugs and snails. They live where their prey lives, in damp places, like around ponds or underneath logs. They follow the slime trails of their prey and then swallow them whole. They don't need to constrict their prey.

Slug-eaters are common in gardens and are harmless. They actually benefit gardeners and farmers by eating slugs and snails that damage plants. They protect themselves from predators by rolling up into a spiral when threatened.

Common slug-eater
Duberria lutrix
(20–40 cm)

Snakes or worms?

Worm or **thread snakes** are among the smallest snakes in the world. They look like shiny earthworms and are totally harmless. They are long and thin, with a small, rounded head and tiny eyes that are almost blind. They have smooth, polished, tight-fitting scales and a protective head scale. These features are adaptations for a life of burrowing underground.

Worm snakes spend most of their time in burrows in loose soil. They will appear after heavy rains, like earthworms do, when their burrows get flooded out. They eat small invertebrates, especially the larvae of ants and termites. They follow the scent trail of ants and termites to their nests and can produce their own scent to put off bites from soldier ants and termites.

Worm snakes are eaten by many predators, such as snakes, birds, mongooses, spiders and scorpions. Snakes, like the striped harlequin snake, feed on worm snakes by catching them in their underground burrows.

Worm (thread) snake
Leptotyphlops species (18–24 cm)
This worm snake feeds on termites and ants.

Striped harlequin snake
Homoroselaps dorsalis (35–55 cm)
This harlequin snake only feeds on thread snakes, which it catches in their underground burrows.

Snakes that have venom

All the snakes from this page to page 195 are venomous. A venomous snake kills its prey with poison. Venom is the liquid that contains the poison. It is secreted in small sacs, called venom glands, in the snake's head. The snake's fangs are hooked up to these sacs.

When a snake bites, venom shoots through grooves or hollows in the fangs and into the blood of the animal. The poison kills or paralyses the prey.

When the **red-lipped herald** is threatened, it flattens its head and flares its lips. It has large back fangs inside its mouth. It paralyses frogs using the venom from its fangs. A herald snake will bite to protect itself but it is not poisonous to humans.

Jelger Herder

Skaapstekers

Some people believe skaapstekers or 'sheep stabbers' bite and kill sheep, which is where they got their name. But they have mild venom that cannot kill sheep and they are not dangerous to humans.

Skaapstekers chase down their prey in the day. They move at great speed. They catch small invertebrates, lizards, frogs and rodents by biting them to inject venom.

Spotted (or rhombic) skaapsteker
Psammophylax rhombeatus (80–120 cm)

More people die from being struck by lightning than from snakebites. There are about 37 venomous snakes out of about 150 different species of snakes living in southern Africa. Of these, only 16 are known to be deadly. Become aware of these snakes by learning about them first. Some of the most dangerous ones are shown over the next few pages.

Quick-moving mambas

Mambas are venomous snakes. They have long bodies and tails and long heads, which are flat on the sides. Herpetologists describe their heads as coffin shaped. They are large, quick-moving snakes and are active during the day. In the mating season, the males wrestle with each other in a fascinating dance called combat dancing. Read about this on page 147.

The most feared and deadly

The **black mamba** is the largest venomous snake in Africa. It is also the most feared and deadly one, as its venom is highly poisonous. Like other snakes it would prefer to move off rather than attack, but if seriously threatened it will bite. It hisses first to warn the enemy or predator. If the enemy does not go away, it will lift up its body and open its mouth wide as a warning that it will strike. The black mamba is not actually black at all but grey-brown to dark grey in colour. It is the lining on the inside of its mouth that is black.

Black mambas live on the ground and hunt birds and small mammals, like rodents and squirrels. They will chase down their prey and then bite many times until the prey is paralysed from the venom. They live in a wide variety of habitats, from dry savanna to forests, but not deserts.

Black mamba
Dendroaspis polylepis
(2.5–3.5 m, up to 5 m)

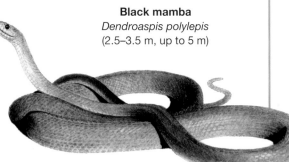

A tree-living mamba

The **green mamba** is smaller than the black mamba and spends most of its time in trees. It even sleeps in trees, high up on a branch. It is brilliant-green in colour, which is excellent camouflage against the leaves. In this way, it avoids being seen by predators and can sneak up on its prey. It mainly eats birds, especially the eggs and chicks, and small mammals like bats and squirrels.

Green mambas are not nearly as deadly as black mambas. Their venom is far less poisonous and a bite from a green mamba rarely causes death, although you must get treatment quickly if bitten. Green mambas are shy snakes and not seen often. They are only found in a few habitats like coastal bush and moist forests.

A green mamba

Arie v.d. Woude (www.shutterstock.com)

Hooded cobras

Cobras protect themselves from predators, such as honey badgers and mongooses, by making themselves look larger and more threatening. They raise the front part of their bodies off the ground and spread their necks to make a hood. If the enemy does not go away, they will strike.

Cobras live on the ground and hunt by chasing their prey. They will also climb into trees in search of food or to bask in the sun. They eat rodents, frogs, lizards, fish, birds and their eggs and chicks, other snakes and even insects. They are mostly active in the day but will also search for food at night.

A spitting cobra

The **Mozambique spitting cobra** spits venom as far as three metres. This is like shooting water through a syringe.

It does this to protect itself from predators. It's very painful if the venom gets in the eyes.

It will also bite. You need to be treated as soon as possible because the venom is very poisonous and can be life threatening.

Spitting cobras have dark bands across their hoods, which are seen when they lift up their bodies. They live in north-eastern parts of southern Africa in savanna habitat.

**Mozambique
spitting cobra**
Naja mossambica
(1–1.5 m)

A deadly cobra

The **Cape cobra** doesn't spit venom. It bites to protect itself. It will try to escape first but if it can't it will rear up and strike. Its main enemy is the honey badger.

The Cape cobra is responsible for the most human deaths caused by snakebites in the South African Cape.

Cape cobras vary in colour. They often match the colour of their environment, which helps with camouflage. They can be light brown to yellow to reddish-brown or black. They live in the south-western parts of southern Africa, in fynbos, karoo and desert habitats.

Cape cobra
Naja nivea
(1–2 m)

Honey badgers feed on highly poisonous snakes, such as Cape cobras and puff adders. Unbelievably, they can survive a bite from one of these snakes!

Slow-moving adders

Adders have short, stocky bodies and triangular-shaped heads. They are not fast movers so they ambush their prey. They eat rodents, birds, lizards and other snakes.

Puff adders

Puff adders bask on paths and rocks in the day so humans often step on them or get too close and are bitten. They are sluggish snakes and don't move off like other snakes if they are disturbed. They '*huff*' and '*puff*' when they feel threatened. Puff adders cause most of the serious snakebites in southern Africa.

Thea Felmore

Puff adders are found in most habitats, except forest and desert.

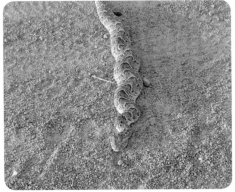

Alan Calenborne

Puff adders move forward in a straight line, a bit like caterpillars, along the ground. They blend in well with the ground. They rely on camouflage to escape predators or hide from prey.

Berg adders

Berg adders are small and like basking in clumps of grass on rocky ledges. They '*puff*' and '*hiss*' to warn enemies that they are ready to strike. There have been no known human deaths from berg adders.

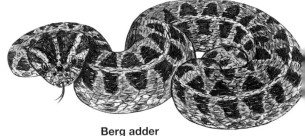

Berg adder
Bitis atropos (20–40 cm)
Berg adders prefer mountainous areas.

Snakes, like most other animals, are found in different places or habitats. This is often one of the ways we learn how to identify them. Read where the two adders on this page are found. Also read more about different habitats on page 138.

Tree-loving snakes

Boomslangs and **vine snakes** live in trees or bushes. They hunt for food here, such as chameleons, lizards and birds. While boomslangs hunt by chasing their prey, vine snakes hunt by ambush. Both snake species blow their necks up first as a warning, and then bite if they feel threatened. They can both be deadly to humans.

Crafty camouflage

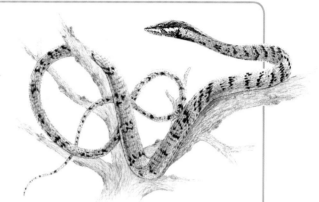

Boomslang (tree snake)
Dispholidus typus (1.2–1.8 m)
The colour of boomslangs varies from mottled-grey in young snakes to brown in females to different shades of green in males. These different colours help to camouflage them from predators and prey.

Vine snake (twig snake)
Thelotornis species (80–120 cm)
Vine snakes have excellent camouflage. They are the colour of bark, are as thin as twigs and they move very slowly.

Binocular vision

The **boomslang** is a large snake with enormous eyes. It has the biggest eyes of any African snake. The **vine snake** has pupils the shape of keyholes.

The special shapes of these snakes' eyes give them binocular vision. Binocular vision allows them to judge distance accurately. For example, it allows them to see how far a branch or prey is away from them. The incredible eyes of these two snakes are adaptations for moving around and hunting prey successfully in trees.

Jelger Herder

Vine snakes have a bright orange tongue but the fork is black tipped. Some herpetologists think that their tongues are used to attract prey, such as lizards, who might mistake the tongue for an insect!

Insects and
other Invertebrates

▶ All about invertebrates

What is an invertebrate?

There is a fascinating group of animals called the invertebrates that live all around us, even inside our homes, but we know very little about them. Invertebrates are animals without a backbone or spinal column. This means they have no skeleton inside their bodies. Instead, they have a hard shell, a hard outer 'skin' called an exoskeleton or a soft inner body cavity filled with water.

Invertebrates include animals such as spiders and scorpions, crabs and lobsters, snails and earthworms. This group of animals also includes all the insects.

This section introduces you to some of the many invertebrate species we find living around us every day. We will introduce you to many of the amazing adaptations and habits they have developed in order to survive. This book does not cover any of the marine invertebrates, only the ones living on land or in fresh water.

CK Willis/LepiMAP/http://lepimap.adu.org.za

This **garden acraea** is often found in people's gardens.

The incredible thing about invertebrates is that up to a million different species have been named and described on Earth. But not all invertebrates have been discovered and some experts reckon there are up to 10 million different invertebrate species on Earth. That's 95% of all animals! All the other animals – all the mammals, birds, frogs and reptiles – make up the remaining 5%.

The value of invertebrates

Invertebrates form a very crucial part of the ecosystem. An ecosystem is made up of plants and animals living together. They interact and work together to make sure that the whole system survives.

A source of food

Invertebrates are food to thousands of other animals. In this way they help them survive.

This **flap-neck chameleon** is feeding on a praying mantis.

Helping others

Invertebrates help humans and other organisms by feeding on pests, such as **mosquitoes**, which suck the blood of humans and animals. Read more about this on page 229. Without **dragonflies** and **damselflies**, which feed on mosquitoes, there might be a lot more mosquitoes around!

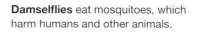

Damselflies eat mosquitoes, which harm humans and other animals.

Pollinating flowers

Invertebrates pollinate flowers as they feed on them. They collect pollen grains on their faces or bodies from the male part of the flower. They move to another flower and smear the pollen grains onto the female part of the flower.

Mountain pride butterflies feed on and pollinate flowers.

Sir David Attenborough, a world-renowned naturalist, said, 'If we and the rest of the back-boned animals were to disappear overnight, the rest of the world would get on pretty well. But if the invertebrates were to disappear, the world's ecosystems would collapse'.

The science in a name

Every invertebrate is given its own Latin (or scientific) name and common (or English) name. The Latin name is used all over the world. It is written in italics. Italic letters slope to the right, *like this*. The common name can vary from country to country. Look at the example below.

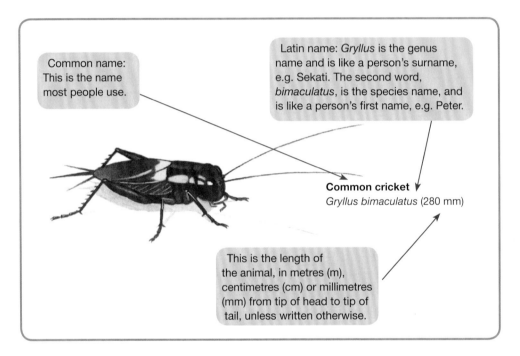

Common name: This is the name most people use.

Latin name: *Gryllus* is the genus name and is like a person's surname, e.g. Sekati. The second word, *bimaculatus*, is the species name, and is like a person's first name, e.g. Peter.

Common cricket
Gryllus bimaculatus (280 mm)

This is the length of the animal, in metres (m), centimetres (cm) or millimetres (mm) from tip of head to tip of tail, unless written otherwise.

Sometimes invertebrates cannot be identified because it's so difficult to tell them apart. In this section, when we don't have a Latin name for an invertebrate, we have given the family name or another group name.

For example, if the species of cricket we are looking at is not known, then we have given the genus name only (*Gryllus*) or the family name (Gryllidae).

- The study of insects is called entomology.
- The study of spiders and scorpions is called arachnology.
- The study of butterflies and moths is called lepidoptery.

Classification helps identification

When we classify an invertebrate, we put it into groups with other animals or invertebrates that have the same or similar features. This helps us identify it.

Invertebrates in the same group are similar – they are like one another. Invertebrates in different groups are different – they are unlike one another. Examples of group names are Genus, Family, Order, Class, Phylum and Kingdom.

To give you an idea of how this works, this is how the **common cricket** is classified:

Kingdom	**Animalia**	This group includes all the animals. Another kingdom would be Plantae, or plants.
Phylum	**Arthropoda**	This group includes all animals with segmented bodies and jointed limbs.
Class	**Insecta**	This group includes all the insects.
Order	**Orthoptera**	This group includes all grasshoppers, locusts and crickets.
Family	**Gryllidae**	This group includes all field crickets, tree crickets and their relatives.
Genus	***Gryllus***	This group includes all the field crickets.
Species	***Gryllus bimaculatus***	This is the common cricket.

The more specific the classification, the more similar the invertebrates are to others in the group. For example, the insects grouped in the **family** Gryllidae are more similar than the insects grouped in the **order** Orthoptera. And these are more similar than the insects grouped in the **class** Insecta.

This system of classification is used all over the world. It's a way to identify and share the information about all the plants and animals found on Earth.

Learning about lifecycles

In a lifecycle there are stages an animal goes through as it grows and changes from an egg to an adult. The changes invertebrates go through are called metamorphosis and happen as the animals grow. Most invertebrates have an exoskeleton, which makes it very difficult for them to grow.

An invertebrate's exoskeleton is like a hard outside skin or skeleton, which supports and protects it. When it gets too big for its exoskeleton, it loses it. This is called moulting. A new, larger exoskeleton is formed. Invertebrates either develop through incomplete or complete metamorphosis.

Incomplete metamorphosis

This is when there isn't a big change from youngster to adult. The nymph is a smaller version of the adult. This is true for ticks, spiders, scorpions, dragonflies, termites, mantises, stick insects, grasshoppers, crickets, bugs and more.

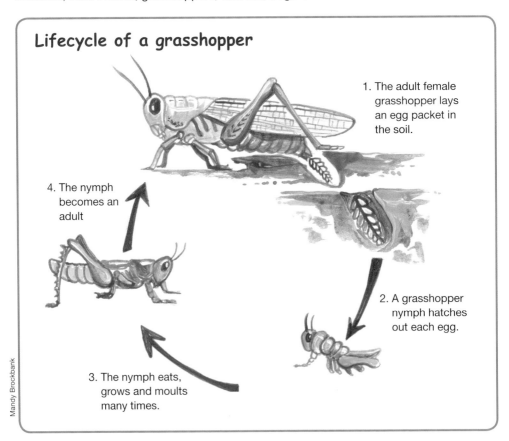

Lifecycle of a grasshopper

1. The adult female grasshopper lays an egg packet in the soil.

2. A grasshopper nymph hatches out each egg.

3. The nymph eats, grows and moults many times.

4. The nymph becomes an adult

Mandy Brockbank

Complete metamorphosis

This is metamorphosis when there is a complete change from youngster to adult. The young larva looks very different from the adult. This is true for beetles, antlions, flies, wasps, bees, ants, moths, butterflies and more.

Lifecycle of a beetle

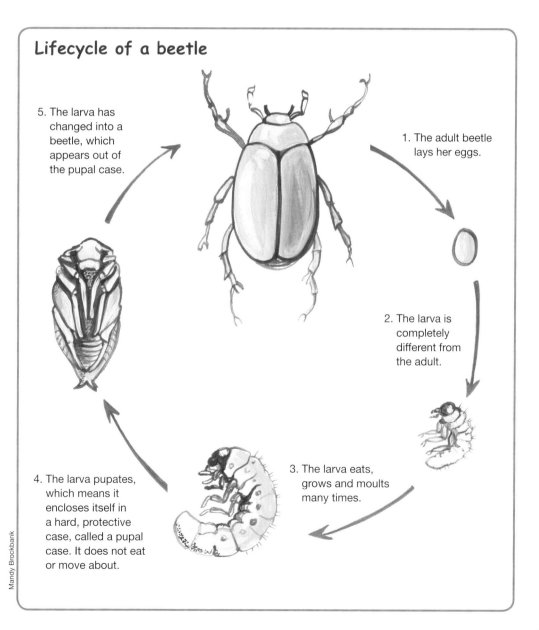

5. The larva has changed into a beetle, which appears out of the pupal case.

1. The adult beetle lays her eggs.

2. The larva is completely different from the adult.

3. The larva eats, grows and moults many times.

4. The larva pupates, which means it encloses itself in a hard, protective case, called a pupal case. It does not eat or move about.

Mandy Brockbank

Amazing adaptations

Adaptation is how an animal's body or behaviour changes over time so that it can survive better in its environment. Here are some examples.

Whirligigs are great in water

Whirligig beetles are well adapted to life in water. They are streamlined and smooth. The back legs act just like oars and are fringed with hairs. They are used for moving rapidly through the water. This helps whirligigs to escape from predators or to catch prey. Their eyes are split in two. The top half looks above the water surface while the bottom half looks below. This means they can watch out for predators in the air and water.

Dung beetles are great with dung

Dung beetles are well adapted to working with dung. Their antennae are like fans. They open and close to smell out dung. The head is shaped like a shovel, for collecting bits of dung together. The front legs are wide and armed with strong teeth for digging and scraping dung.

Lynne Matthews

Dragonflies are great in the air

Dragonflies are well adapted for hunting prey. They have large, well-developed eyes used for spotting prey. Their wings are strong and powerful so they can fly fast. Their legs are like baskets designed for scooping prey out of the air.

Lynne Matthews

Escaping predators

One of the biggest worries for invertebrates is to avoid being eaten! They have found many ways to do this. Here are a few …

Nocturnal living

Many invertebrates are nocturnal, such as **praying mantises**. This means they are active at night and sleep or hide during the day. They do this to avoid daylight, when it's far easier for predators to spot them.

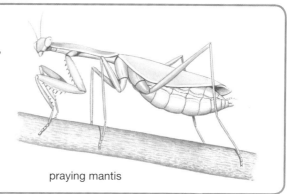

praying mantis

Intelligent colours

The colouring of some invertebrates helps them to escape predators. **Bladder grasshoppers** are green to blend in with green plants, making them invisible to predators. **Elegant grasshoppers** use bright colours to warn predators that they are toxic to eat.

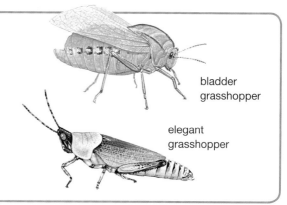

bladder grasshopper

elegant grasshopper

Social living

Some bees, wasps and ants live in large, well-organised colonies. They are called social insects. One reason for living in a group is better protection against predators. One animal has less chance of being eaten in a group. A group is also much better at defending itself against a predator than one animal.

Lynne Matthews

Paper wasps ready to defend their nest.

Conservation matters

Conservation came about because so many animals and plants were disappearing from the Earth. Conservation is a way of looking after and taking responsibility for the natural world.

What are the problems?

- Invertebrates are losing their habitat! There are so many people and so much development that there are fewer and fewer places left for the invertebrates to live.

- Humans use chemical herbicides to kill weeds and pesticides to kill insect pests. But these affect many others plants and animals, not just the ones they're intended for.

- Alien plants, such as black wattles, lantana and Port Jackson, are replacing our indigenous vegetation and the invertebrates are losing their food and habitat. Alien plants are plants that don't belong in southern Africa. They come from other countries.

lantana

black wattle

Port Jackson

These alien plants take over and replace the natural vegetation. As a result, many invertebrates and other animals disappear.

One of the rarest butterflies in the world!

There are only about 100 **Brenton blue** butterflies left. The development of houses along the coast has destroyed its habitat. Now, this butterfly is only found in one place in South Africa. Conservationists had to protect this place by starting a special reserve called the Brenton Blue Butterfly Reserve. The reserve is in Brenton-on-Sea, near Knysna in the Western Cape.

Brenton blue

Try this organic pesticide recipe! Mix together with water: chopped up khakibos, some dishwashing soap, and a dash of Jeyes fluid. Leave to stand overnight. Spray on your garden pests.

How can you help?

- Find ways of turning your garden into an attractive place for invertebrates, such as starting a butterfly garden. Bringing invertebrates into your garden will bring birds, frogs and reptiles, even mammals if you are lucky. Look at http://www.buglife.org.uk/getinvolved/ for more ideas.

- Take out alien plants and plant indigenous flowers, shrubs and trees. Get your school or community involved.

- Use organic pesticides rather than chemical ones that don't break down but stay in our gardens for a long time, harming the plants and animals.

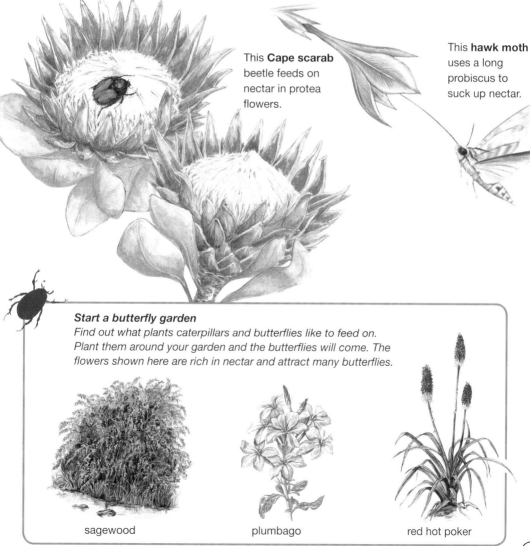

This **Cape scarab** beetle feeds on nectar in protea flowers.

This **hawk moth** uses a long probiscus to suck up nectar.

Start a butterfly garden
Find out what plants caterpillars and butterflies like to feed on. Plant them around your garden and the butterflies will come. The flowers shown here are rich in nectar and attract many butterflies.

sagewood

plumbago

red hot poker

▶ The insects

How do we tell insects apart from the other invertebrates?

Insects are invertebrates because they don't have a backbone or spinal column. But they are different from other invertebrates because they have their own unique set of features. Look at the picture of the longhorn beetle below to see this.

If you find an animal that has all the features listed below, then you will know that the animal is an insect. Have a look at some of the other invertebrates on pages 246–259 in this book. They are not insects. They are relatives of the insects, like their cousins.

How do you recognise an insect?

a body that is divided into a head, thorax and abdomen

Lynne Matthews

two antennae (or feelers) used for smelling and touching

a hard outer 'skin' called an exoskeleton

three pairs of legs

Grasshoppers and crickets

What's that sound?

The insects in this group make amazing sounds by rubbing their different body parts together. They rub their wings or their legs together or their wings against their legs. This is a bit like rubbing your finger up and down a comb. They use the sound to attract a mate, tell others of their territory or to warn predators.

Escaping predators

Many invertebrates use camouflage to hide from predators. Often they are bright green and hang around in bright green vegetation.

Lynne Matthews

This **grass katydid** is camouflaged in the grass. Katydids all have very long antennae.

Lynne Matthews

This little grasshopper nymph is hiding in the grass. The nymph is one stage in the lifecycle of the grasshopper. Look at the grasshopper lifecycle on page 202.

Common garden crickets

Common or **field crickets** are known by their chirping at night in our gardens. They tunnel under the lawn. The males sit at the entrance to their burrows and rub their wings together to attract the females.

Garden crickets are very clever. When you look for them, they muffle their chirrup as you get close. This makes it seem like they are far away and helps them to escape predators.

These crickets eat plants, but they can chew holes in your clothes if they get into your house.

Common cricket (field cricket)
Gryllus bimaculatus (2.8 cm)

King of the crickets

Most people are scared of **king crickets** because they are so large, red and grotesque looking! Their heads are big for their bodies and they have a pair of huge, curved jaws. They produce a horrible-smelling black liquid to frighten off predators. They come out at night to feed, but you can dig them out of their burrows during the day, when they hide.

They eat plants and other insects. They especially like slugs and snails and therefore help humans by keeping their numbers down. Hadedas are enemies of king crickets and love to gulp them down! King crickets rub their body plates together to make a sound.

King cricket (Parktown prawn)
Family Stenopelmatidae (1.5–5.5 cm)

A cricket's ears are on its legs. You can spot a cricket's ears by looking for a single white dot near the bend of each front leg. A grasshopper's ears are in its abdomen.

Hollow grasshoppers

The unusual thing about male **bladder grasshoppers** is that their bodies are almost completely hollow and filled with air, like big air sacs. The air sac acts as a resonance box. As the grasshopper rubs its legs up and down the sides of its body, it makes the call louder and it carries further. The sound it makes is a long, loud rasping call that sounds more like a big bullfrog than a small grasshopper.

The female's body is like a normal grasshopper's body, but she cannot hop or fly.

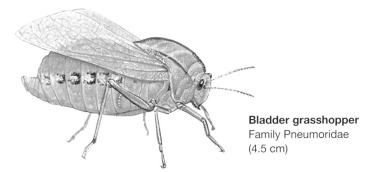

Bladder grasshopper
Family Pneumoridae
(4.5 cm)

Toxic grasshoppers

Toxic grasshoppers produce substances that can harm other organisms. They are brightly coloured, often yellow, red or black, to warn predators. This is their main means of defence! They often taste terrible and smell awful. Many are poisonous. After a first taste, a young bird or baboon will quickly learn not to choose this type of food again.

If badly handled, the **elegant grasshopper** produces a yellow liquid that has a bad smell. They can be a huge pest in some areas, when they swarm as they eat and destroy crops.

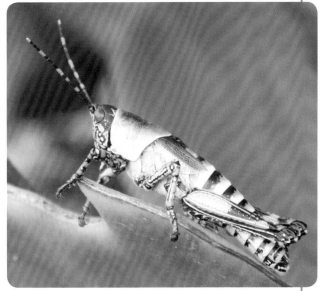

Carol Broomhall

Elegant grasshopper *Zonocerus elegans*
(1–11 cm)

Dragonflies and damselflies

Dragons and damsels

Dragonflies and **damselflies** live at the edges of ponds and streams. They are usually first spotted darting around the water. The males protect a territory around the water by attacking or chasing away intruders. You might also spot them away from water as they often wander off to search for prey or hide from predators.

Both dragonflies and damselflies catch insects in flight. They have large, well-developed eyes and very mobile heads used to search for prey. Their legs are not used for walking but for perching, and the stiff hairs on their legs form a basket to scoop insects out of the air.

What is the difference?

You can tell dragonflies and damselflies apart by looking at their wings when they are resting. Dragonflies spread their wings out, while damselflies fold their wings together.

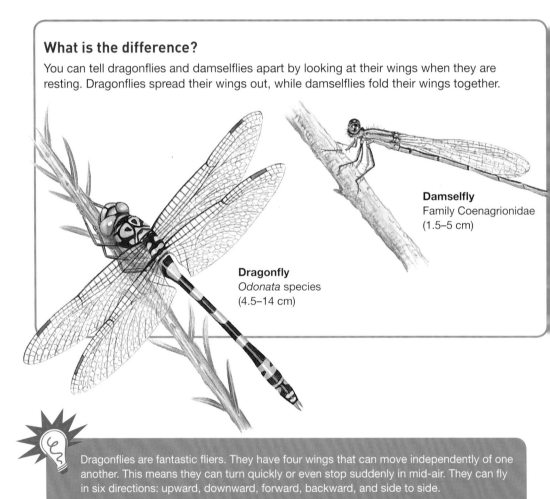

Damselfly
Family Coenagrionidae
(1.5–5 cm)

Dragonfly
Odonata species
(4.5–14 cm)

Dragonflies are fantastic fliers. They have four wings that can move independently of one another. This means they can turn quickly or even stop suddenly in mid-air. They can fly in six directions: upward, downward, forward, backward, and side to side.

A mating dance

Dragonflies and damselflies have a lovely mating dance. When the male is ready to mate, he grabs hold of the female just behind her head. They will fly together like this in tandem for some time. The female then bends her body forward and grasps the male to collect his sperm. They will stay like this for as long as 15 minutes.

When they are finished mating, the female lets go and they go back to the tandem position. In some species, the males carry on holding onto the female while she lays her eggs. This is to guard her against predators.

male

female

Brian Valentine (http://www.flicker.com/photos/lordv)

Damselflies hold onto each other while mating, making a circular or heart shape with their bodies.

Learning about lifecycles

Both dragonflies and damselflies lay their eggs in water. The female lays her eggs by skimming over the water surface and dipping her abdomen into the water. Some lay their eggs inside plants hanging in the water by making small slits in them.

The eggs hatch into nymphs. The nymphs have gills like fish and live in the water. They are carnivorous and eat other insects, such as mosquitoes and flies. They moult several times as they grow. When they are ready to become adults, they crawl out of the water, their exoskeleton splits and an adult dragonfly or damselfly emerges. Read more about lifecycles on pages 202–203.

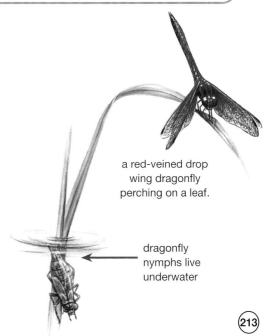

a red-veined drop wing dragonfly perching on a leaf.

dragonfly nymphs live underwater

Termites

Termite colonies or superorganisms

Termites live in colonies of thousands of individuals. They all work together to support the colony. They act as one individual or **superorganism**. Individuals can't survive on their own for long.

This is like people playing in a soccer or hockey team, where each member must do his or her job for the team. The team won't survive without its players and the players are nothing without their team. In a termite colony there must be 100% cooperation or the colony won't survive.

Some termite colonies build mounds, called termitaria.

Who lives in a termite colony?

- **Soldiers** protect the colony and have large pincers.
- **Workers** find and collect food and have small pincers. They feed the queen, build and repair the nest and look after the eggs and young.
- The **queen** is up to 10 cm long and spends all her time laying eggs.
- The **king**'s job is to mate with the queen.
- The **winged termites** are the males and females who leave the colony to mate and start new nests.

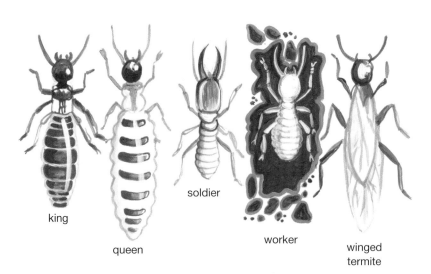

king

queen

soldier

worker

winged termite

Inside a termitaria

The worker termites build the **chimneys** for ventilation. The chimneys keep the nest cool. This is like air conditioning.

There are **tunnels** leading to the outside and sources of food, such as wood and grass.

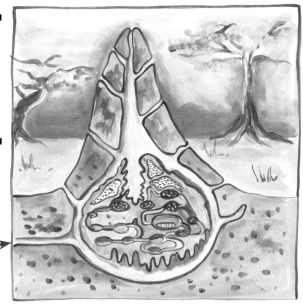

Mandy Brockbank

The **nest** is made up of shelves and chambers. The king and queen live in the royal chamber. This is surrounded by fungus gardens, which are grown by the worker termites to feed the whole colony. The eggs and larvae are looked after in other chambers.

Building termitaria, such as this large one, is an incredible achievement for tiny termites. The worker termites that build these are less than a centimetre big (about 5–8 mm). The conditions inside the termitaria are warm and moist, which is perfect for growing fungus gardens.

Termites are huge pests around buildings, as they can destroy anything made out of wood. But they are very important recyclers of dead wood. They enrich the soil, and they feed many animals, such as aardvark.

Aardvark have large, strong claws for breaking open termitaria.

Mound-building termites

Common termites build termite mounds, sometimes as high as seven metres. They are often covered in plants or large trees because the termites take the seeds into the nest, where they sprout. These mounds are made up of a number of passageways that lead to the termite nest at the base of the mound.

The worker termites are vulnerable to ants, birds and many other predators while searching for food on the ground. To reach food, usually wood or timber, they build tunnels of mud on the surface of the soil. This protects them by keeping them hidden as they move to and from the nest. If you break open these mud tunnels, you will expose the termites and they will run around trying to find cover. If you continue watching, you will see the termites start to rebuild their tunnels with little mud balls they make with saliva and soil.

Termites benefit many animals, such as dwarf mongoose and warthog, which use old termite mounds to make a den.

This is a nest built by **common termites**.

Underground termites

Harvester termites do not build mounds. Their nests are underground and consist of tunnels and chambers. You know you have these termites in your garden by the small piles of loose soil they push out when building their home. The worker termites have eyes and thick skin as they come to the surface to harvest grass for food.

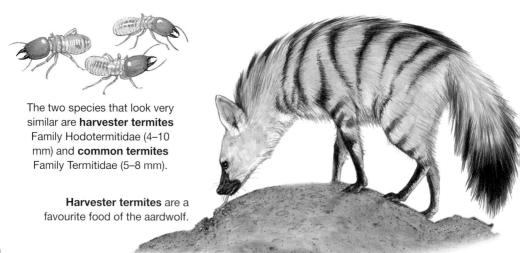

The two species that look very similar are **harvester termites** Family Hodotermitidae (4–10 mm) and **common termites** Family Termitidae (5–8 mm).

Harvester termites are a favourite food of the aardwolf.

Antlions

Hidden hunters

Antlion larvae are masters at trapping ants. They build small hunting pits in dry, sandy soil. The antlion larva hides at the bottom of the pit under the sand, waiting for an ant to fall into the pit. As soon as the larva feels an ant struggling inside its trap, it grabs the ant with its large jaws (called chelicerae) and then drags it under the sand. The jaws are also used to pierce the ant's body and suck out the body fluids.

Antlion adults look similar to **dragonflies** but they have club-shaped antennae like you see in the picture. Dragonflies, on the other hand, have small, thread-like antennae that you may hardly notice (see page 212). Adult antlions prey on smaller insects at night. During the day, they hide in shady, wooded places.

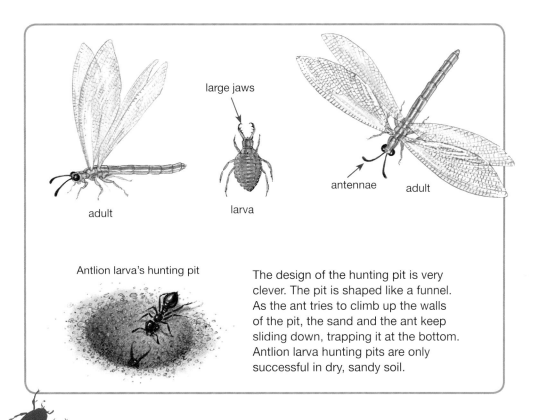

large jaws

adult

larva

antennae

adult

Antlion larva's hunting pit

The design of the hunting pit is very clever. The pit is shaped like a funnel. As the ant tries to climb up the walls of the pit, the sand and the ant keep sliding down, trapping it at the bottom. Antlion larva hunting pits are only successful in dry, sandy soil.

If you find an antlion pit, use a grass stalk to tickle the bottom of the pit. The antlion might think it is an ant and grab hold of the stalk. Quickly pull it out and have a look. It's very different to the adult.

Bugs

Real bugs

Although you might call any insect a 'bug', the invertebrates in this group are the real bugs! They all have mouthparts adapted for piercing and sucking. The mouth is a beak-like tube that is used to suck up liquids. They live on the sap of plants or the blood of other animals or humans.

Lynne Matthews

Shield bugs are armed with stink glands to chase off predators. They feed on the sap of plants.

Amazing relationships

Aphids have an amazing relationship with ants as they excrete sweet plant sap that is called honeydew that ants love to eat. You can watch an ant go from one aphid to the next, tapping the honeydew from their rear ends.

The ants prod the aphids with their feelers to release the honeydew. In return, the ants protect the aphids from predators, such as **ladybirds**, by bugging them until they go away. Aphids are pests to farmers and gardeners as they weaken plants and spread disease among the plants.

aphid

ladybird

Lynne Matthews

Aphid Family Aphididae (1–2 mm)
Ladybirds prey on aphids.

aphid

ant

Pugnacious ants visit aphids for their honeydew. Read more about them on page 233.

Shrilling calls

Cicadas are known for their loud, shrill calls during summer in the mating season. They are among the loudest insects around! But they are very hard to find as they are so well camouflaged. They are similar in colour to the bark of the tree they are sitting on. It's also confusing because they all call at once from various trees in the same area.

If you do eventually find one, you will usually see a few more in the same tree. They feed by sticking their tube-like beak (or mouth) into the tree to suck up the tree's sap.

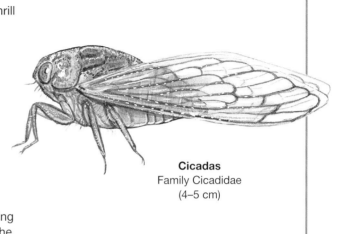

Cicadas
Family Cicadidae
(4–5 cm)

Scorpion-bugs

Water scorpions creep slowly around muddy ponds and the bottom of shallow streams. They look for nymphs, tadpoles, small crabs and mosquito larvae to eat.

They use the tips of their tails for breathing air on the surface of the water. They use their front legs for grabbing and holding their prey, like scorpions do.

They have a short, curved beak, used for sucking out the body contents of their prey.

Water scorpion
Family Nepidae
(up to 10 mm)

Praying mantises

Praying predators

It's easy to recognise a **praying mantis** because their front legs are folded forward as if they are praying. Their front legs are an important part of their hunting strategy, which is the way they hunt and catch their food. All mantises are carnivorous, which means they only eat other animals.

Mantises are nocturnal. This helps them to escape being eaten by other predators, such as birds and reptiles, which are active in the day. Most of them have camouflage colours to blend in with the vegetation.

Praying mantis Order Mantodea (40–85 mm)

Patient hunters

Praying mantises are incredibly patient predators. They stalk their prey, usually a flying insect, slowly and gradually, waiting for the right moment to strike. When the prey flies close enough, the mantis shoots out its front legs with lightning speed and grabs hold of it.

Their front legs have rows of sharp spines, which are used to grip prey. They have large eyes and a very moveable head for closely following the prey's movement. The females usually eat the male during or after mating. This fattens her up to help with egg production.

Stick insects

Stick mimics

Stick insects are fascinating. Their bodies have changed or adapted to look just like sticks, twigs or grass stems. This is called mimicry. Mimicry is when an animal copies or takes on the appearance of another organism. They do this to protect themselves from predators.

Stick insects even sway slightly like twigs or grass stems caught in the breeze. They cannot fly or jump and so are very helpless if a predator does find them. If this happens, they freeze and play dead, as most predators won't eat dead food. Stick insects are only active at night, which also helps them to escape being eaten by ants, frogs, lizards and birds. Stick insects only eat plants.

Lynne Matthews

Stick insect Order Phasmatodea (10–250 mm)
This stick insect has frozen on a tree, hoping to become invisible and escape danger.

Beetles

Beetle brilliance

Worldwide, beetles are by far the largest and most diverse group of insects. About 370 000 beetle species have been described Of these, about 18 000 species are found in South Africa and there are many more undescribed!

All beetles have a hard, protective shield covering their backs. These are actually hardened front wings, called elytra. The elytra protect and cover the back wings, which are used for flying. All beetles have chewing mouthparts, unlike bugs, which have sucking mouthparts. See bugs on page 218.

hard elytra cover a beetle's back and protect the wings underneath

large mouthparts used for chewing

Anna Ekstein

Giant longhorn beetles eat wood, leaves, roots and pollen.

Hose-nose cycad weevil

The female **hose-nose cycad weevil** has an incredibly long thin snout. The male's snout is far shorter. The female uses the tip of her snout to drill holes through cycad cones to reach the seeds on the inside. Then she lays batches of eggs on the seeds. When the larvae hatch, they feed on the seeds.

Anna Ekstein

Long snouts

Weevils are a very successful group of beetles. They have a long snout used to drill holes into plants to lay their eggs. They make up the largest animal family. There are 45 000 species of weevil worldwide! They are so successful because the larvae and pupae develop inside the plant tissues and are quite safe from predators, parasites and bad weather.

Lynne Matthews

The strongest animal is a beetle!

Rhinoceros beetles are the strongest animals on earth! That's in relation to their size, of course. They can carry 850 times their own weight. This is like one rhino carrying 850 rhinos on its back! While the male rhinoceros beetle carries a large horn on his head like a rhino, the female only has a small bump.

The males use their horns to fight over females. They also use their horns for digging into the ground to hide from predators or into rotting material, such as your compost heap, where they lay their eggs. The adults feed on nectar, plant sap and fruit.

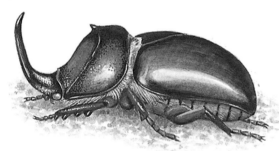

Rhinoceros beetle
Family Scarabaeidae
(1–4.5 cm)

Whirling water beetles

Whirligig beetle bodies are well adapted to water life. They whirl around on top of the water like ice-skaters. To breathe underwater, they take a bubble of air with them, which sits on the end of their tails or is trapped under their wings.

To avoid predation they live in groups, because one animal has less chance of being eaten in a group.

They prefer pools in gently flowing streams. The current often brings them their food.

They eat other insects and tadpoles. Read more about their adaptations on page 204.

Whirligig beetle
Dineutus grossus (13–14 mm)

Beetles grow and develop through complete metamorphosis. This means they change from eggs to larvae to pupae to adults. See the beetle lifecycle on page 203.

Dung-shovellers

As their name tells us, **dung beetles'** lives are all about dung! They eat dung for food and use it to feed their young. Some dung beetles roll dung balls, lay their eggs in them, and bury them under the ground. Others lay their eggs in the dung heap or in the soil underneath the dung.

Their lifecycle is shown on the opposite page. They grow and develop through complete metamorphosis. Read more about this on page 203, and read how well adapted they are to shovelling and rolling dung on page 204.

Dung beetle
Family Scarabaeidae
(10 mm–5 cm)

Dung beetles help the environment

- They clean up the environment by collecting and burying dung.
- They carry nutrients under the soil that feed the plants.
- They help to scatter the seeds of plants that land up in the dung after passing through the stomachs of herbivores.
- They help with germination by taking the seeds below the ground.

The **Addo flightless dung beetle** is only found in a small area in the Eastern Cape. It is recognised as a vulnerable species because it depends mostly on elephant and buffalo dung for survival. But these large herbivores are losing their habitat to humans and their numbers have declined. Flightless dung beetles only produce one egg or young beetle a year.

Addo Elephant National Park, SANParks

The lifecycle of a dung beetle

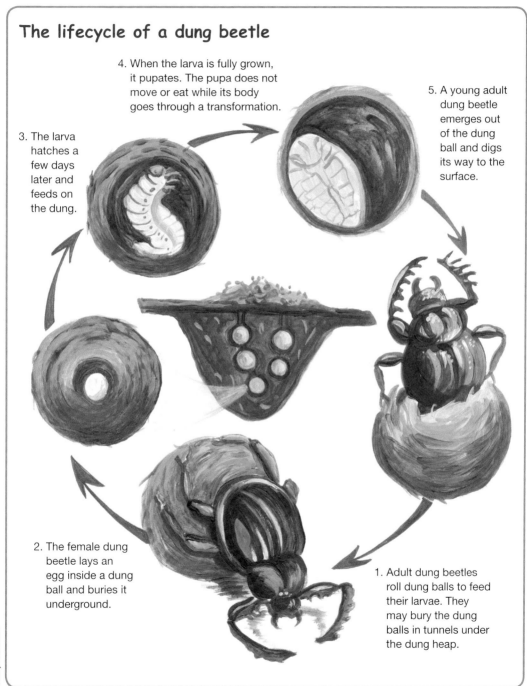

4. When the larva is fully grown, it pupates. The pupa does not move or eat while its body goes through a transformation.

5. A young adult dung beetle emerges out of the dung ball and digs its way to the surface.

3. The larva hatches a few days later and feeds on the dung.

2. The female dung beetle lays an egg inside a dung ball and buries it underground.

1. Adult dung beetles roll dung balls to feed their larvae. They may bury the dung balls in tunnels under the dung heap.

Mandy Brocktbank

A gardener's enemy

We usually see these **rose beetles** in our gardens feeding on the flowers. They are called rose beetles because they cause a lot of damage to roses. They are also called fruit chafers because some bore holes into ripe fruit and feed on the juices. As you can imagine, they are not particularly liked, especially by fruit farmers.

The large white grubs living in your compost heap might be the larvae of these beetles. The females lay their eggs here and the larvae feed on the compost.

Rose beetle (fruit chafer)
Family Scarabaeidae
(1–7 cm)

Poisonous beetles

Look out for these **blister beetles**. Their bright colours tell us and other animals, such as birds and lizards, that they are actually poisonous. The poison is called canthardin, which is kept in the beetle's body and tastes terrible. It can also blister the skin.

We often see the adults sitting on flowers, which they eat. Have a look at the blister beetle's lifecycle on the opposite page.

Blister beetle
Family Meloidae
(2–5 cm)

Some blister beetles lay their eggs in flowers. The hatched larvae then hitch a ride with a visiting honeybee back to its nest. In the nest there is a honeybee egg feast waiting for them!

The lifecycle of the blister beetle

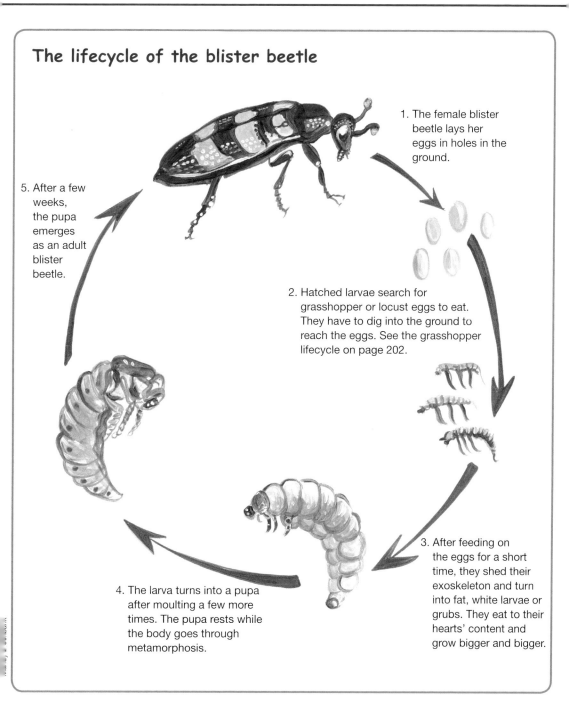

1. The female blister beetle lays her eggs in holes in the ground.

5. After a few weeks, the pupa emerges as an adult blister beetle.

2. Hatched larvae search for grasshopper or locust eggs to eat. They have to dig into the ground to reach the eggs. See the grasshopper lifecycle on page 202.

3. After feeding on the eggs for a short time, they shed their exoskeleton and turn into fat, white larvae or grubs. They eat to their hearts' content and grow bigger and bigger.

4. The larva turns into a pupa after moulting a few more times. The pupa rests while the body goes through metamorphosis.

Flies and mosquitoes

Incredible aviators

Flies and mosquitoes are different to all other insects because they only have one pair of wings. The hind (or back) wings of this group have become little knob-like structures that help with balance during flying.

Flies are the most incredible aviators. They can make a 90-degree turn in 50-thousandths of a second. That's faster than a human eye can blink! Can you imagine an aeroplane doing that?

Lynne Matthews

Dean Gruyt

Bee flies often have patterned wings. There are over 1 000 species of bee fly in southern Africa. The adults only eat nectar.

Flies eat nectar, plant sap, blood, other insects and dead matter. A fly can taste its food using its feet.

Why do we chase flies off our food?

Flies cannot chew because they don't have teeth so they have to digest food outside their bodies. They do this by pouring enzymes onto the food from their mouths. The food dissolves and they suck up the soup with their straw-like tongues and sponge-like mouthparts.

Flies spread germs by landing on food before we eat it. They pick up germs from one place, like a garbage can, and carry the germs somewhere else. When they vomit up enzymes, they pass on the germs.

What do you know about mosquitoes?

Although most people dislike mozzies, they usually don't know very much about them. They are actually very interesting insects to get to know! It's the females that suck blood. They need the blood to develop their eggs. The males only feed on the nectar of flowers or the juices of ripe fruit.

Mosquito
Family Culicidae (4–10 mm)

The lifecycle of the mosquito

1. The female mozzie lays her eggs in standing water and the eggs glue together to form a floating raft, called a culex.

5. The adult emerges out of the pupa.

breathing trumpets

siphon

4. When full grown, the larva turns into a pupa and floats on the surface of the water, breathing air through breathing trumpets.

3. Each larva feeds and moults many times, as it grows bigger.

2. The eggs hatch and the larvae float on the water's surface to breathe air though a siphon or tube. They wriggle about if you move standing water which is where mosquitoes prefer to lay their eggs.

Mosquitoes that carry malaria belong to the Family Anophelinae. Malaria is a disease that kills millions of people all over the world every year. Malaria is passed on when a mozzie sucks the blood of one person infected with malaria and then later sucks the blood of another person. Malaria is passed through the mozzie's saliva.

Flying assassins

Robber flies are not really robbers. They are brilliant, flying assassins. They chase down other flying insects on the wing, grab hold of them with their legs, and stab them with their powerful proboscis. Their large eyes mean they have excellent vision and their movable heads can turn to look for prey. They eat flies, bees, wasps, beetles, dragonflies, moths and butterflies.

Some robber flies are excellent mimics ('copycats') of carpenter bees. Read about carpenter bees on page 236. They hang around the entrance holes of a bees' nest and then grab an unsuspecting bee.

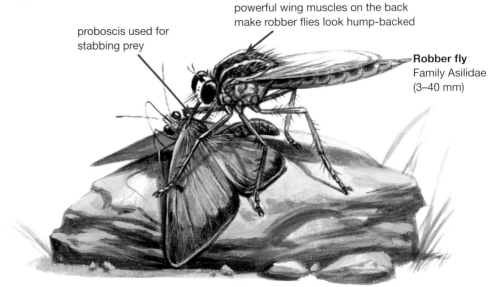

proboscis used for stabbing prey

powerful wing muscles on the back make robber flies look hump-backed

Robber fly
Family Asilidae
(3–40 mm)

Experts in sanitation

Blowflies may seem to lead a disgusting lifestyle but they are experts at sanitation. The adult blowflies lay their eggs in animal carcasses. The eggs hatch quickly and the white larvae or maggots eat whatever is left of the carcass, leaving only the bones. They do this by dissolving or digesting the meat with their saliva and then sucking up the meaty 'soup'.

Blowflies play an important role in breaking down carcasses and cleaning up the veld. Without them, there would be a lot of rotting, stinking meat left lying around.

Blowfly larvae, called maggots, feed on the bodies of dead animals

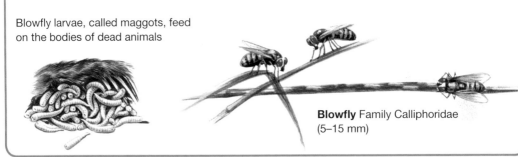

Blowfly Family Calliphoridae
(5–15 mm)

Ants, bees and wasps

Insects with a sting

This is the third-largest group of insects after butterflies and moths (see page 239). There are over 120 000 different species in the world. They have two pairs of membranous wings that are joined together by little hooks. Some of them have lost their wings, like some wasps and worker ants, although there are winged ants that leave the ant colony to mate. Read more on page 214.

Each insect in this group has a hardened tip on the end of its abdomen, which is used for piercing, sawing or stinging.

Honeybees are very important pollinators of flowers. They also turn flower nectar into honey. Read more about them on pages 235–236.

Tree-nesting ants

Most **cocktail ants** are arboreal, which means they live in trees. You can recognise the cocktail ant by the way it lifts its abdomen straight up when alarmed. Some cocktail ants build nests in trees, called carton nests. They are made of chewed plant fibres and saliva. If their nest is bumped or broken, the ants stream out with their abdomens raised. They defend their nest by biting or wiping a poisonous substance that comes out of the ends of their abdomens onto the attacker. They have a sting but hardly ever use it.

Cocktail ants love sugary food, so they form relationships with sap-sucking bugs, such as aphids. See pages 218 and 243.

Cocktail ant
Crematogaster species
(4.5 mm)

Ants on the move

Army ants live in ant colonies under the ground. But they are better known for the way they appear in masses above the ground. Sometimes up to 50 million ants can march together! They are called driver ants because of the way they drive out everything as they move.

Army ants march in thick columns in search of food. They eat everything in their path, such as caterpillars, beetles and grasshoppers. They also raid termite nests. The larger soldier ants march on the outside of the column and defend the smaller worker ants on the inside. The soldiers have large heads and pincer-like jaws and give an extremely painful bite.

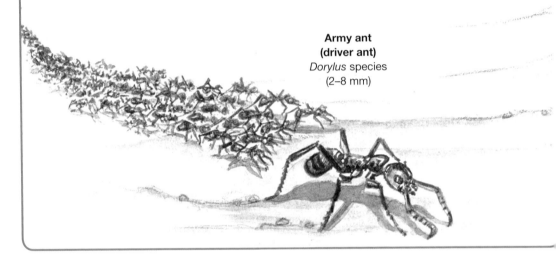

**Army ant
(driver ant)**
Dorylus species
(2–8 mm)

Winged ants

In the mating season, winged males and females leave the army ant colony to mate. Read more about them above. The winged males are called **drones**. They are much bigger than the soldier ants. You might have seen them in the garden. They are totally harmless.

A drone mates with a queen and dies soon after. The queen finds a good place to start a new ant colony. She drops her wings and then digs a new hole to lay her eggs in.

Drones (winged males)
Dorylus species (3–4 cm)

Ant colonies are also sometimes described as superorganisms. This means that an ant can't survive on its own. They need to live and work together in a group to survive.

Fierce protectors

Pugnacious ants are active and aggressive. They won't hesitate to attack you if you stand close to their nest hole. They bite and then hang on with their sharp jaws. They often get humans jumping and running away! They form large colonies underground. You can spot the entrance to their nest by the small round holes with soil spread out away from the hole.

Pugnacious ants mostly eat insects but they also eat honeydew secreted by aphids. In return, they protect the aphids from predators. Read more about this on page 218.

This is the nest hole of **pugnacious ants**. They take plant seeds into their nest underground, where they germinate in warm, moist conditions.

Pugnacious ant
Anoplolepis custodiens (5–10 mm)

Alien ants

The **Argentine ant** comes from South America. It is considered to be among the world's 100 worst animal invaders! It has invaded many parts of southern Africa. Argentine ants push out indigenous ants, such as cocktail ants, which other animals depend on. Read about this on page 243.

Argentine ants also eat the oily parts of seeds on the ground and then leave the seed there. The seeds die instead of germinating underground, which is where other ants take them. Some animals, like lizards, depend on indigenous ants for food and lose their food supply when Argentine ants take over.

Argentine ant
Linepithema humile
(2–3 mm)

233

The life of honeybees

Honeybees are fascinating to study. They live in large colonies made up of the queen (who lays up to 1 000 eggs a day), 7 000 to 50 000 female worker bees, and drones (the males that mate with the queen).

The life of the worker bee is spent searching for nectar, pollen and water. The worker bees tell one another where they can find food by doing a special bee dance. Can you believe the bee dance tells the direction, distance and amount of food they have found?

Spotted aloe
Aloe affinis

Worker bees collect nectar and pollen to feed the bee colony

Honeybees
Apis mellifera
(15 mm)

Anna Ekstein

Great providers

Honeybees are very important to humans and many other animals. They provide many things we use:

- **Honey:** Worker bees turn flower nectar into thick honey in the honey sacs in their bodies.
- **Beeswax:** Worker bees secrete beeswax to make the waxy honeycomb, which is where the honey is stored. Beeswax is used to make wax products like candles and seals.
- **Pollen:** Worker bees collect pollen to feed the bee larvae. People use the pollen as a health supplement.
- **Royal jelly:** The bee larvae that are to become queens are fed royal jelly. Royal jelly is full of vitamins.

Honeybees on their waxy honeycomb. Honey mixed with pollen is stored in each cell to feed the bee larvae.

Beekeeping

Beekeepers provide a place for a bee colony to live and store their honey. Here a beekeeper is capturing a wild colony of bees.

The beehive is made up of wooden frames, like the one the beekeeper is holding. The bees build a wax honeycomb in each frame. They store their honey in small cells in the honeycomb. See opposite for what the cells of a bee nest look like.

Carol Broomhall

A beekeeper
at work

Badger-friendly honey

You can buy badger-friendly honey! Honey badgers are often killed by beekeepers because they destroy beehives to eat the bee larvae and honey. Honey with a label saying 'badger-friendly' means that the beekeeper has found better ways to stop honey badgers from destroying their beehives.

Honey badger

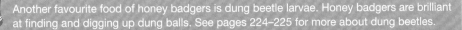

Another favourite food of honey badgers is dung beetle larvae. Honey badgers are brilliant at finding and digging up dung balls. See pages 224–225 for more about dung beetles.

Wasps without wings

Velvet ants are actually female wasps and give a very painful sting. But they don't have wings and they can't fly. They have a fine coat of hair that makes them look velvety.

The female walks around looking for the nests of bees, ants or wasps. Once in the nest, she lays her eggs on the larvae. The larvae become food for the velvet ant larvae when the eggs hatch. The lifecycle of the velvet ant is completed inside the bee's nest. Ants, bees and wasps develop through complete metamorphosis. Read what this means this on page 203.

Velvet ant
Family Mutillidae
(15–17 mm)

Woodworkers

Carpenter bees are large, black bees with bands of yellow or white hairs on them. They are not social bees like the honeybee. Rather, they live on their own.

They are called carpenter bees because the female bores long tunnels about 15 cm deep into soft, dry wood using her powerful jaws. She divides the tunnel up into many cells using wood shavings and saliva. She supplies each cell with food, which is a yellowy, pasty mixture of pollen and nectar. Then she lays a large, white egg on the food. The eggs hatch into larvae, which then feed on the mixture. The larvae pupate inside the cells, until finally the adults appear out of the tunnel. Read more about lifecycles on pages 202–203.

Carpenter bee
Family Xylocopinae
(10–35 mm).
A carpenter bee bores tunnels
in wood that lead to its nest.

Fascinating relationships

Fig wasps have a fascinating relationship with fig trees, like the swamp fig in the picture. They depend on one another for survival! There are tiny male and female flowers hidden inside fig tree fruit. Female fig wasps dig their way into fig fruit. Once inside, she lays her eggs in the female flowers. When the eggs hatch, the wasp larvae feed on the flowers and grow.

The female wasp helps the fig tree by pollinating the female flowers with pollen she has collected from the male flowers of another fig fruit. In this way, the wasp and the tree benefit from each other. Fig wasps are the only species that pollinate fig trees, while fig wasps can only breed inside fig tree fruit.

actual size of the fig wasp

fig fruit

branch from a swamp fig tree

the only way in is through a tiny hole in the top

Fig wasp
Family Agaonidae
(1–4 mm)

Read more about invertebrate lifecycles on pages 202–203. Wasps develop through complete metamorphosis as they change from a youngster into an adult.

Without fig wasps pollinating the flowers of fig trees, there would be no more fig trees. Fig trees are beautiful big trees. They provide homes, food and shelter for monkeys, birds, bats and many other animals.

Paper nests

Paper wasps are social wasps, which means the males and females live together. Females build their nests out of plant fibres they gather from plant stems and dead wood, which they mix with saliva. You may have seen their paper nests hanging under your roof.

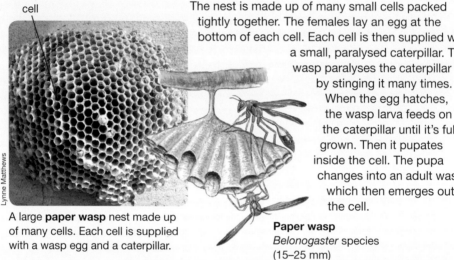

cell

The nest is made up of many small cells packed tightly together. The females lay an egg at the bottom of each cell. Each cell is then supplied with a small, paralysed caterpillar. The wasp paralyses the caterpillar by stinging it many times. When the egg hatches, the wasp larva feeds on the caterpillar until it's fully grown. Then it pupates inside the cell. The pupa changes into an adult wasp, which then emerges out of the cell.

A large **paper wasp** nest made up of many cells. Each cell is supplied with a wasp egg and a caterpillar.

Paper wasp
Belonogaster species
(15–25 mm)

Mud nests

Mason wasps live by themselves. They make their nests out of a mixture of mud and regurgitated water. Females either build their own nests or they use existing holes, such as beetle tunnels in wood, keyholes or even old nail holes around buildings.

Mud chambers, called cells, are built inside the nest and an egg is laid in each chamber. Adults feed their young in the same way as paper wasps. The whole lifecycle is completed within the mud chamber.

This mason wasp nest has been made in a keyhole.

Mason wasp (potter wasp)
Odynerus species (25 mm)

Butterflies and moths

Insect beauties

This is the second-largest group of insects after the beetles. Read about beetles on pages 222–227. There are over 100 000 different species of butterflies and moths in the world. They all have sucking mouthparts and tiny scales covering their wings. The 'dust' that comes off on your fingers if you try to hold a butterfly is its tiny scales. Be careful or it might not be able to fly again!

The scales give the wings their colour, which is used for camouflage or attracting a mate. The sucking mouthparts are like a long tube, a bit like an elephant's trunk. It is called a proboscis. The proboscis is used for sucking up nectar, fluids or moisture. When the butterfly is not using its proboscis, it coils it up under its head, like in the photo below.

CK Willis/LepiMAP/http://lepimap.adu.org.za

African monarch
Danaus chrysippus
(60–70 mm)

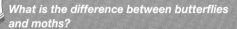

What is the difference between butterflies and moths?

- *Butterflies are usually active in the day and moths at night.*
- *Butterflies rest with their wings closed above their body while moths rest with wings folded flat.*
- *Butterflies are usually more brightly coloured than moths.*
- *Butterflies have club-shaped antennae while moths often have feathery antennae.*

CK Willis/LepiMAP/http://lepimap.adu.org.za

Emperor moth *Epiphora* species

Lifecycle of the African monarch butterfly

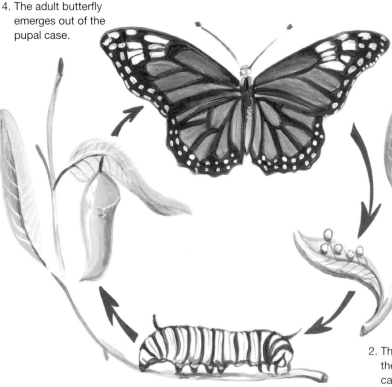

4. The adult butterfly emerges out of the pupal case.

1. A butterfly lays her eggs on a food plant that she knows the caterpillars would like to eat.

2. The eggs hatch and the caterpillars, also called the larvae, spend their whole lives eating, moulting and growing. To moult means to shed or lose the outer skin or exoskeleton as they grow bigger.

3. The caterpillar forms a pupa called a chrysalis that does not eat or move while it goes through metamorphosis. In **butterflies**, the chrysalis is not protected by a cocoon and hangs from something, like a branch. In **moths**, the pupae are protected by a cocoon or they are unprotected under or on the ground.

Mandy Brockbank

The number and diversity of butterflies found in a habitat is an excellent way of telling us how healthy an ecosystem is. For example, if the ecosystem is healthy, then there will be a great number and diversity of butterflies in the habitat.

Migratory butterflies

The **brown-veined white** and **African migrant** are two butterfly species that migrate, often in their millions! They are seen all over southern Africa. Lepidopterists think they migrate to look for better feeding grounds. When there are so many of them they eat up all the food plants in the area. Food plants are the specific types of plants they eat. They then have to move on to find more food. They always fly in the same direction, north-east, and usually in summer and autumn. They are not really 'migrating', because migrating means to return to the area you left. They keep flying until they die!

Brown-veined white
Belenois aurota
(wingspan: 45–50 mm)

African migrant
Catopsilia florella
(wingspan: 60–65 mm)

Butterflies prefer different habitats

To identify a butterfly it often helps to know what kind of habitat it prefers. Read what a habitat means below. The brown-veined white prefers open country like open woodland and grassland. The African migrant is found in all habitats except desert.

Loot Eksteen

The yellow pansy prefers savanna and grassland habitats and is often seen in gardens.

A habitat has a particular kind of vegetation (like grassland, forest, woodland or desert), climate (weather), topography (the lay of the land), geology (the type of rock found there) and group of animals.

Poisonous butterflies

Predators mostly avoid the **African monarch** butterfly. This is because the caterpillars feed on milkweed plants, which contain poisonous, milky latex. The caterpillars store this substance in their bodies, which makes them and the adult butterflies taste terrible to predators. Monarch butterflies like most habitats.

African monarch (milkweed butterfly)
Danaus chrysippus (wingspan: 50–70 mm)

Lemon tree-lovers

The **citrus swallowtail** is a lovely, large butterfly that is often attracted to citrus plants in your garden, like lemon, lime and orange trees.

The female lays her eggs on the leaves of these plants, as the caterpillars like to eat them. Citrus swallowtails like any habitat, except deserts.

Citrus swallowtail *Papilio demodocus*
(wingspan: 70–90 mm)

Mountain beauties

Table Mountain beauties prefer open rocky areas in mountainous, grassy habitats. They are very fond of red flowers. They ensure the survival of the red disa as they are the only known pollinator of this flower. A food plant of the caterpillars is thatch grass.

Table Mountain beauty (mountain pride)
Aeropetes tulbaghia
(wingspan: 70–80 mm)

Red disa
Disa uniflora

Opals and ants

Opal butterflies belong to a group of butterflies called Lycaenids. They need cocktail ants to complete their lifecycle. The ants protect the caterpillars from predators. In return, the caterpillars give the ants sweet honeydew to eat. Read more about cocktail ants on page 231.

This **cocktail ant** is getting honeydew from a Mooi River opal caterpillar.

Bietou
Chrysanthemoides monilifera

The **common opal** prefers living on the coast in the Western Cape. It flies around sand dune bushes. The caterpillars feed on the leaves of the bietou plant. This butterfly is disappearing because coastal development is destroying its habitat. Poisons used in gardens and agriculture also kill this butterfly.

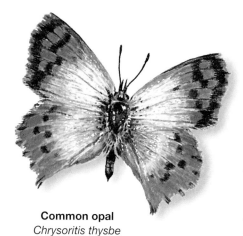

Common opal
Chrysoritis thysbe
(wingspan: 30 mm)

The **Mooi River opal** prefers grassy, mountain slopes where there are rocky outcrops. They are only found in KwaZulu-Natal and Mpumalanga.

Mooi River opal *Chrysoritis lycegenes* (wingspan: 24 mm)

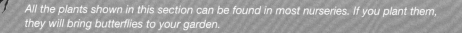

All the plants shown in this section can be found in most nurseries. If you plant them, they will bring butterflies to your garden.

243

Marching caterpillars

The caterpillars of the bagnest moth walk in long lines called processions, each one holding onto the other. They are called **processionary worms**. They can look like long snakes, which may put off predators!

When they find the plant they prefer to feed on, they bunch up together on the tree trunk or shrub. When its time to pupate, they each spin a silken cocoon, which is enclosed in a tough outer covering called a bag nest. This makes it very difficult for predators to get to them.

Processionary worms
(caterpillars)
(5 cm)

Horn-eating caterpillars

Have you ever seen the horns on an antelope or buffalo skull with worm-like towers sticking out of them? These are towers of cemented caterpillar droppings made by horn moth caterpillars as they tunnel into the horn.

The **horn moth** lays her eggs on dead antelope horns. The larvae hatch and tunnel into the horn as they feed on it. The towers are formed from the caterpillars' droppings. When fully grown, the caterpillars pupate within these towers. The adult moths emerge from the ends of the towers. Hundreds of caterpillars may live on one horn.

Horn moth
Ceratophaga vastella
(wingspan: 11–14 mm)

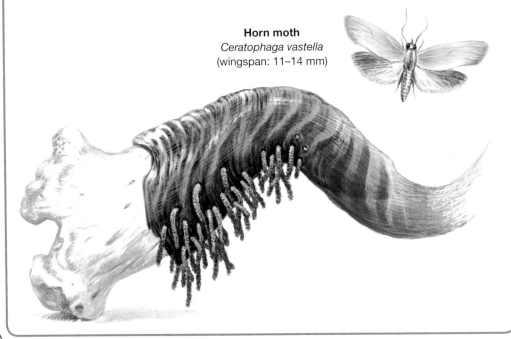

Owl-like moths

You can recognise this **cream-striped owl moth** by the large eyespots on its wings. Lepidopterists think the eyespots are used to scare off predators as the moths might appear to be large owls flying at night. They have also found another way to escape predators. When hunting them they can hear the high-pitched sounds that bats make, which humans can't hear.

Owl moths are drawn to our lights at night and we often see them resting on the walls of houses. They have been known to land on a person's glass to sip the sweet juice or wine.

Cream-striped owl moth
Cyligramma latona
(wingspan: 62 mm)

Hawk-like moths

Hawk moths have narrow wings and streamlined bodies, which make them strong, fast fliers. The **convolvulus hawk moth** hovers over flowers. It uses its proboscis, which is like a long, thin straw, to suck up the nectar inside flowers. The proboscis is coiled up under the head when not in use.

The larvae or caterpillars feed on the leaves of morning glory creepers. When fully grown, the caterpillars leave the plants to pupate in soft soil under the ground. They don't spin a cocoon. The adult moths emerge out of the pupa.

Wild morning glory
Ipomoea crassipes

Convolvulus hawk moth
Agrius convolvuli (wingspan: 8 cm)

Moths develop through complete metamorphosis.
Find out what this means on page 203.

▶ Other invertebrates

What are they?

The rest of this section will now introduce you to some of the other invertebrate groups. These animals are all invertebrates, like the insects are. But they are not insects because they don't have insect features! Read about insects on page 208.

The bodies of the relatives of the insects are organised differently from insect bodies. Snails, slugs, earthworms, scorpions and spiders are some examples. These animals are put in separate groups because they don't have too much in common.

We have only included some of the land-living invertebrates. There are also many marine invertebrates, such as octopuses, starfish, sea snails, crabs, lobsters, mussels and oysters.

Slugs are like snails but without a shell or with a very reduced shell. A slug's body is mostly made of water and it dries out easily if exposed to the sun.

It travels on an enlarged foot and secretes slime on which to move. This protects the foot and stops it from slipping. The slime trail is also a way of telling other slugs where and who it is.

Deon Guyt

Snails

Giant snails

Giant land snails are the largest snails in the world. They can grow up to 20 cm long. Like other snails, their hard shells protect them from predators. The shell also stops them from drying out in the sun because it holds moisture on the inside.

Giant land snail
Achatina species (13–20 cm)

They have a big muscular foot for moving around. They come out at night to eat but bury themselves under the ground during the day. They search for plants, fruit and vegetables to eat. Sometimes they also eat stones, bones or even concrete, which contains the calcium they need for hardening their shells.

Giant land snails can live up to ten years. Many people keep them as pets, but they have become pests in places where they don't belong. In America it is illegal to keep them because they destroy crops.

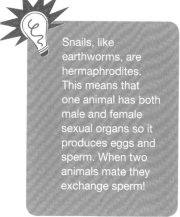

Snails, like earthworms, are hermaphrodites. This means that one animal has both male and female sexual organs so it produces eggs and sperm. When two animals mate they exchange sperm!

The shells of giant land snails are often found lying on the ground.

Lynne Matthews

Earthworms

Life under ground

Earthworms spend most of their lives underground. Their long, muscular bodies are divided into rings with tiny, stiff hairs on the bottom. Earthworms burrow through the soil using the muscles along their bodies, their slimy skin and their tiny hairs. As they move through the soil, they eat plant matter mixed with soil.

Their droppings have many nutrients, which enrich the soil. This benefits plants. Earthworms also mix and aerate the soil, which helps plants' roots to grow.

The giant earthworm is one of the longest earthworms in the world. One of them set a record at 6.7 metres in length! Normally they grow to about 1.8 metres, but that's still incredibly long.

This is called a saddle or clittelum. The saddle produces an egg case, rich in nutrients, for housing the earthworm's eggs.

Giant earthworm
Microchaetus species (1.8 m)

Wizzard worms (http://www.wizzardworms.co.za)

Start your own wormery

Many people set up their own wormeries at home. They feed the earthworms vegetable waste, cardboard and plant material. In return, the earthworms' droppings provide very rich compost. People feed the compost to their plants, which helps them to grow and flower.

Worm urine drains out of the wormery and into the jug. It is diluted with water and sprayed on plants.

Millipedes and centipedes

Friendly detritivores

Millipedes are lovely, harmless invertebrates. Many people know them as songololos. They are detritivores, which is the name given to animals that eat dead and decaying leaves, wood and other plant matter.

Millipedes escape predators by writhing around if they are touched. They also roll themselves up into tight, hard coils. Their hard exoskeleton helps to protect their soft body and legs. If this doesn't work, they produce toxic substances, which taste horrible or will burn a predator's skin and eyes. Very few birds or monkeys will go near them but certain animals, such as African civets, love eating millipedes. Civet dung is often full of millipede rings.

Millipedes have two pairs of legs on each body ring. They can have up to 200 pairs of legs.

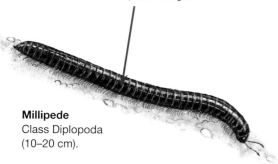

Millipede
Class Diplopoda
(10–20 cm).

A coiled millipede protects itself from predators.

Fearsome predators

Centipedes are quite fearsome predators. They hunt insects, earthworms, snails and other invertebrates at night. Many people are frightened of them because they can bite. Their bite is more painful and longer lasting than a bee sting. Centipedes have long antennae on their heads for feeling around in the dark. They also have a pair of claws on their heads for grabbing prey. The claws have glands for injecting poison into their prey and paralysing them.

During the day, they hide in dark, damp places, such as under leaves, logs and stones. They also hide in garden sheds or around buildings. They are very flat so they hide well.

Centipedes have one pair of legs on each body ring. They have about 25 pairs of legs.

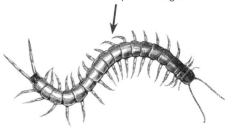

Centipede Class Chilopoda
(1–12 cm)

Spiders

What makes up a spider?

While most insects have six legs, spiders have eight. Most spiders also have eight eyes. But more eyes don't mean better eyesight! They can only see changes between light and dark and quick movements around them.

Other senses, like touch and taste, are more important to spiders. They kill prey with a bite from their poisonous fangs. They have no teeth so prey has to be made into a liquid so they can suck it up. They do this by pumping enzymes out of their mouths and onto the prey to dissolve it.

Super webs

Spiders have a special way of catching food. They spin webs, snares and traps out of silk. Silk is incredibly strong but very light in weight. It has been estimated that a line of silk long enough to wrap around the world would only weigh 450g!

Spiders also build egg sacs, like cocoons, out of silk to house their eggs. Young spiders, called spiderlings, scatter themselves by ballooning into the wind on silk threads.

A **golden orb-web spider** on its web. Read more on the opposite page.

Webs of golden silk

The female **golden orb-web spider** spins a very large, strong spiral web of golden silk for catching flying insects. The web is so strong it can even trap small birds. It hangs between trees or in the corners of buildings.

The female hangs upside down in the centre of the web while the male hangs on the outer edges. She is huge compared to him. He steals the food she catches. He mates with her when she is feeding just in case she decides to eat him! The female lays her eggs in an egg sac buried in the ground.

Golden orb-web spider
Nephila species (25–30 mm)

Many different spiders build orb-shaped webs. Orb-webs are spiral in shape. Read on page 252 how spiders do this.

Bark-like spiders

Female **bark spiders** build large orb webs up to 1.5 metres wide. They build them at night to catch their food. The webs stretch from one tree to the next. Bark spiders are very hard to see during the day because they hide so well. They rest on the branch of a tree and bunch their legs up tightly to their bodies.

Their body colouring plus the two 'horns' sticking out of their bodies makes them look like the bark or thorns of trees. It's very difficult for predators to see them. The males are tiny and very little is known about them.

Bark spider
Caerostris sexcuspidata
(8–30 mm)

Spiders benefit humans by feeding on insect pests, such as flies. They also benefit many bird species, which use their spider webs to bind their nests.

How does an orb-web spider construct her web?

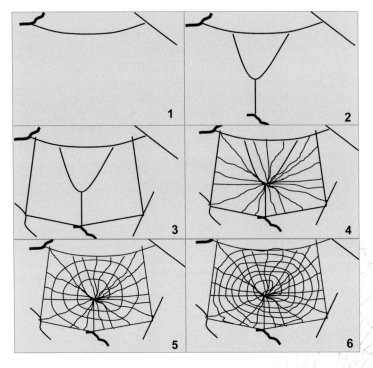

Orb-web spider on its completed web.

1. The spider starts the web by throwing a sticky thread to the wind. If it sticks on a good spot, the spider walks back and forth on the line, making it stronger with new line. The thread becomes a bridge.
2. The spider makes a Y-shaped thread by dropping a line from the bridge and attaching it onto another good spot below.
3. The spider drops more threads from the bridge to make a frame.
4. Then the spider makes many strands that stretch from the centre outwards.
5. It then makes circular, non-sticky threads.
6. The spider lays sticky, circular threads between the non-sticky ones. Then it removes the non-sticky ones.

Nocturnal orb-web spiders build a new web every night. They eat the old web as this is a good source of protein.

Baboon spiders

Baboon spiders are named after their large brown, hairy bodies. They are also known as tarantulas because, like tarantulas, they get very big. They build burrows into the ground and line them with silk. Then they sit and wait at the entrance for prey to pass by. The spider feels if something is coming because it stretches the silk beyond the entrance of the burrow. When prey steps on the silk, the spider grabs it and drags it down into the burrow. They eat a variety of invertebrates, lizards and frogs.

When a male is ready to mate, he will often wander around looking for a female. If he were to wait for a female to pass by, he might wait forever! The female places her egg sac at the bottom of the burrow. She protects the eggs and spiderlings until they disperse. Baboon spiders can give humans a very painful bite.

Lynne Matthews

spinneret – the silk gland that produces silk

Fishing spiders

Fishing spiders live close to water and hunt from the water's edge. They don't make spider webs. They feel for the movement of passing prey with the tips of their legs. Then they dive into the water and wrestle with their prey until they have trapped it. They also run on the surface of the water to chase after prey. They can breathe underwater by trapping air in their body hairs.

They eat a variety of invertebrates, frogs, tadpoles and small fish. The female looks after her egg sac by carrying it around with her until the eggs hatch.

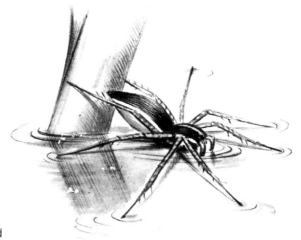

Fishing spider
Thalassius spinosissimus
(15–30 mm)

Scorpions

What makes up a scorpion?

Scorpions, like spiders, have eight legs but they also have a pair of pincers, which spiders don't have. While spiders use a web to catch and hold prey, scorpions use their pincers.

They are active at night, when they hunt for insects, millipedes, centipedes, snails, spiders, scorpions, reptiles and mice. You should wear shoes at night when you are walking around outside so you don't step on a scorpion. During the day, scorpions hide under rocks, bark, logs or in crevices. If you are scorpion-hunting, this is where you should start looking, but be extremely careful!

Carol Broomhall

This thin-tailed scorpion, the **Cape burrowing scorpion**, uses its large pincers for catching and killing prey.

Thin-tailed or thick-tailed?

Scorpions are frightening animals because they have stings and some are deadly. But you need to understand scorpions so you know what you are dealing with.

Scorpions can be split into two groups. The first group is made up of the **thin-tailed scorpions**. They have thin tails and weak venom. They use their large, powerful pincers to catch and kill prey. The second group is made up of the **thick-tailed scorpions**. They have large tails and powerful venom. A sting from their tail is highly venomous. They use their tails to catch prey. The venom then paralyses or kills the prey.

See if you can spot the two different groups of scorpions – thin-tailed and thick-tailed – over the next few pages.

Burrowing scorpions

This **shiny burrowing scorpion** spends most of its time hidden underground in its burrow. It digs a long, deep tunnel, as much as one metre deep. It uses its mouthparts to dig and its front legs to scrape back the soil. It sits at the entrance to the tunnel and waits for prey, such as crickets and other insects, to pass by. It then runs out and grabs them.

It has broad, powerful pincers used to catch prey and crush it to death. If the prey is very large, it is stung and held until it dies. This scorpion stings to protect itself. The sting is painful but not deadly to humans.

Shiny burrowing scorpion
Opistophthalmus glabrifrons
(5–12 cm)

Rock-loving scorpions

Zulu flat rock scorpions have flat bodies and long, thin tails. This allows them to squeeze between narrow cracks and crevices of rocks, where they form dens. In fact, they only live where the rock type can split to form small cracks. They escape from predators into these narrow cracks. It's hard to reach them there.

They have special claws on their feet, which they use for gripping and climbing over the rocks. They catch prey using their large, powerful pincers. Their pincers are also used for protection and can give you a painful pinch. They do have venom glands in their tail but the venom is mild and harmless.

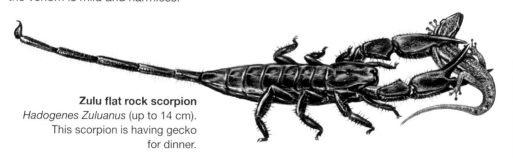

Zulu flat rock scorpion
Hadogenes Zuluanus (up to 14 cm).
This scorpion is having gecko
for dinner.

Dangerous scorpions

Transvaal thick-tailed scorpions kill their prey by stinging them with their large, thick tails. The sting causes paralysis and death. They also use their sting to protect themselves from predators. To this scorpion, humans are predators, so humans may get stung at night, when scorpions are most active. That's why it is better to wear shoes when out walking in the bush.

Fortunately, very few people die from this scorpion's sting because there is such a good supply of antivenom. Read how antivenom is produced below. Nevertheless, you don't want to find yourself in this predicament. It helps to know that thick-tailed scorpions prefer hot, dry places, particularly deserts. They are not found everywhere. They like sandy, gritty soil and dig burrows under stones and logs.

Transvaal thick-tailed scorpion
Parabuthus transvaalicus (up to 14 cm)

Eric Ythier

The mother **Transvaal thick-tailed scorpion** protects her babies by carrying them on her back.

Antivenom is produced by injecting the venom of a scorpion or snake into a sheep, horse or rabbit. The animal produces antibodies to fight the poison. The antibodies are then removed from the blood of the animal, purified and stored to treat scorpion stings.

Sun spiders and whip scorpions

It looks like a spider, but it's not a spider!

Sun spiders are not true spiders. They cannot make silk and don't have poison glands like spiders. Sun spiders chase down their prey using their long, spindly legs. They are active at night, and are usually spotted racing at top speed across the ground.

They have very large, powerful mouthparts that are like small pincers with many teeth. They use these to kill their prey and mash it up. They eat termites, beetles and other insects, and sometimes even lizards. It looks like they have ten legs, but the first pair are not really legs at all. They are used for climbing and catching flying prey out of the air.

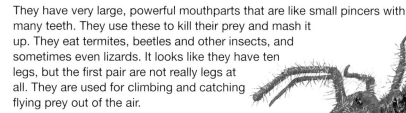

Sun spider (red roman spider)
Family Solifugidae (20–50 mm)

It looks like a scorpion, but it's not a scorpion!

These extraordinary-looking invertebrates are totally harmless. The front legs of the **tailless whip scorpion** are like long whips, which constantly move about. They are used for feeling their way around at night and to find prey.

During the day, they hide in crevices in trees, buildings or underneath rocks. They are so flat it looks like a book has flattened them. This means they can hide in places other predators cannot go. They eat insects, millipedes, slugs and worms. They have large, spiny pincers used for grabbing and holding prey.

Tailless whip scorpion
(amblypigid) *Damon variegates* (up to 25 mm)

Ticks

Blood-sucking parasites

Ticks are parasites, which means that they live or feed off other organisms and cause them harm in some way. As most people know, ticks, such as the **heartwater tick,** attach themselves to mammals and suck their blood. The male has a hard shield over his entire back, while the female only has a small shield around her head. The rest of her body is very elastic so that she can swell up while drinking large amounts of blood. She needs this food for reproduction.

When ticks bite people, they leave a red spot that can itch for days. When an infected tick bites a person, the spot turns black and is surrounded by a large, red swelling. If you get tick bite fever, you will feel ill, have a headache, get a fever, and your body will ache. It takes about five to seven days for these symptoms to show after you have been bitten. You should see a doctor.

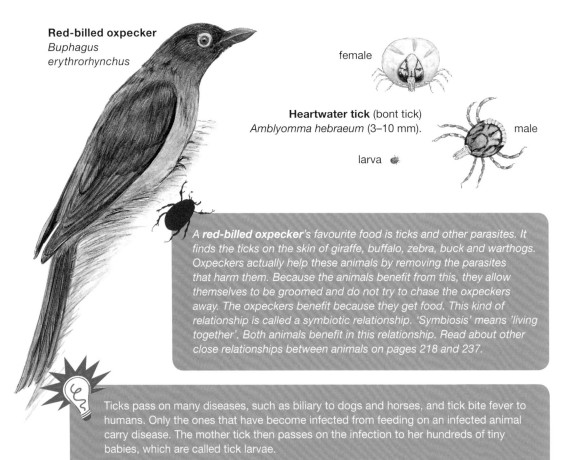

Red-billed oxpecker
Buphagus erythrorhynchus

female

Heartwater tick (bont tick)
Amblyomma hebraeum (3–10 mm).

male

larva

A ***red-billed oxpecker***'s favourite food is ticks and other parasites. It finds the ticks on the skin of giraffe, buffalo, zebra, buck and warthogs. Oxpeckers actually help these animals by removing the parasites that harm them. Because the animals benefit from this, they allow themselves to be groomed and do not try to chase the oxpeckers away. The oxpeckers benefit because they get food. This kind of relationship is called a symbiotic relationship. 'Symbiosis' means 'living together'. Both animals benefit in this relationship. Read about other close relationships between animals on pages 218 and 237.

Ticks pass on many diseases, such as biliary to dogs and horses, and tick bite fever to humans. Only the ones that have become infected from feeding on an infected animal carry disease. The mother tick then passes on the infection to her hundreds of tiny babies, which are called tick larvae.

Lifecycle of the tick

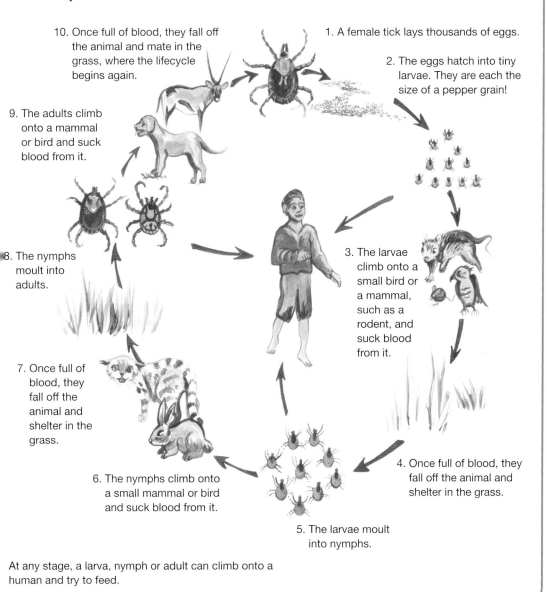

10. Once full of blood, they fall off the animal and mate in the grass, where the lifecycle begins again.

1. A female tick lays thousands of eggs.

2. The eggs hatch into tiny larvae. They are each the size of a pepper grain!

9. The adults climb onto a mammal or bird and suck blood from it.

8. The nymphs moult into adults.

3. The larvae climb onto a small bird or a mammal, such as a rodent, and suck blood from it.

7. Once full of blood, they fall off the animal and shelter in the grass.

6. The nymphs climb onto a small mammal or bird and suck blood from it.

4. Once full of blood, they fall off the animal and shelter in the grass.

5. The larvae moult into nymphs.

At any stage, a larva, nymph or adult can climb onto a human and try to feed.

What kind of lifecycle do ticks have? Do they develop through complete or incomplete metamorphosis? Find out on pages 202–203.

Glossary,
References
& Index

▶ Glossary

abdomen, abdomens – the back part of the three parts an insect is divided into

acute – strong and sensitive

adapt, adaptations, adapted – how an animal's body or behaviour changes over time so that it can survive better in its environment

adaptable – when a species adapts well to its environment; fits in well

aerate – to bring air into a substance

alien plants – plants that don't belong in southern Africa; exotic plants

antelope – fast-running mammals with long legs, hooves and horns, such as impala and bushbuck

antennae – feelers

antibodies – what your body produces to fight sicknesses

anti-predator tactics / strategy – ways to avoid being eaten

anti-venom – medicine used to treat bites or stings from animals like scorpions or snakes

assassins – murderers

aviators – fliers

bask, basking – lying in the sun

bind – to glue; tie together

birds of prey – birds that catch and eat live prey, with powerful beaks and talons

blood vessels – a network of tubes that carry blood around the body

blunt – not sharp or pointed

browser, browsers – herbivores that mainly eat from trees and bushes

camouflage, camouflaged – a way of hiding that makes an animal look like its surroundings

capsule – a covering or envelope in which seeds or eggs develop in plants and animals

carcass, carcasses – the body of a dead animal

carnivores / carnivorous – animals that mainly eat other animals

carrion – the rotting flesh of dead animals

cavity – a hollow space

cells – compartments, chambers

chambers – spaces inside the nest, like rooms in a house

chisel – hand tool with a flat steel blade for wood working

chrysalis – the stage a butterfly goes through between being a larva and an adult

cocoon, cocoons – the casing some larvae make around themselves while changing into an adult

colony, colonies – groups of the same species living together

compete, competing, competition – to contest for food, space or mates

constrict, constriction – when a snake wraps its body around its prey and squeezes until the prey can't breathe and then dies

court – the behaviour animals use to attract a mate

courtship – how animals behave to attract mates

crevices – narrow cracks or splits in rock

critically endangered – at extremely high risk of becoming extinct in the wild

damsels – young women

decaying – dying, rotting

defecate, defecates – to get rid of solid waste from the body

defence, defences – things that provide protection against attack

dense – thick

digest, digesting – breaking food down in the body

disembowel – remove the stomach, intestines and other organs

disperse – to scatter

display, displays – when an animal shows itself or makes itself seen

diverse, diversity – when there are many different kinds or species

dome-shaped – shaped like half a ball

dominance – when one animal is stronger and fitter than others in a group

dominant – the strongest and fittest in a group or area

ecosystem – formed by plants and animals interacting with one another in their environment

elytra – the hardened front wings of beetles

endangered – at high risk of becoming extinct in the wild

endothermic – able to keep the same warm body temperature no matter what the surrounding temperature is

enzymes – a chemical produced by plants and animals

estuary, estuaries – where a river flows into the sea

evaporates – when a liquid becomes a gas

excrete – to get rid of waste matter out of the body

exoskeleton – an insect's hard outer skin or skeleton

exotic – not indigenous; from another country

extinction, extinct – when there are no more of a certain species alive; no longer in existence

faeces – solid waste produced by the body; dung

fangs – hollow or grooved teeth for handling venom

flexible – able to bend easily

formidable – impressive and frightening

foster – not the real mother

frugivores – animals that eat mainly fruit

germinate, germination – sprouting from a seed to a plant

glands – organs in the body that produce a substance

glide – to fly without flapping

gregarious – forming groups; sociable

grotesque – ugly; gross

gut – tube carrying food away from the stomach

habitat – the type of environment a species prefers to live in

herbicides – poisons used to kill weeds

herbivores – animals that mainly eat plants

herpetologists – scientists who study frogs and reptiles

hibernate, hibernating, hibernation – a sleep-like state some animals go into during winter

hierarchy – a system where animals in a group are organised into levels, from lowest to highest

hinge, hinges – a joint that holds two body parts together, and allows them to open and close

horizontally – parallel to the ground

horny – rough and hard

hover – to stay in one place in the air

impaling, impale – spearing

incubate – when eggs are kept warm until they hatch

indigenous – native or local; not exotic

insulate – to stop heat being lost

interlocking – joined by parts that connect or lock into other parts

intertwine – to twist together

intra-African – within Africa

invertebrates – animals without a backbone like insects, spiders, earthworms and snails

larva, larvae – the young form of invertebrates, fish and frogs after they have hatched

latex – a white liquid

lepidopterist – a person who studies butterflies

lifecycle – a series of changes or stages that happen to a plant or animal during its life

ligaments – body parts that hold bones together

mammals – animals that have hair, are warm blooded, whose babies are born alive (not from an egg) and who feed on their mothers' milk

manoeuvre – to move easily in many directions

marshy – made up of soft, wet land

membranous – transparent; see-through

metamorphosis, metamorphoses – the change or transformation of an animal's body as it grows from a youngster into an adult

migrate, migrating – moving long distances from one place to another in search of food or warmth

mottled – spotty; blotchy

moult, moulting – to shed or lose part of its body; birds lose their feathers, mammals lose their hair and invertebrates lose their external skeletons

mucus – a thin, slimy substance

muffle – to make a sound that is not so easy to hear

murky – dark and muddy

musky – smelling strong and sweet

nectar – sugar-rich liquid

nectarivores – animals that eat mainly nectar

nocturnal – active at night

nutrition, nutrients – substances found in food that animals and plants need to grow

nymph, nymphs – the young form of invertebrates that hatch and develop through incomplete metamorphosis

omnivores – animals that eat plants and animals

ornithologists – people who study birds

Palaearctic – Europe, Africa and Asia, north of the tropics

pans – shallow holes in the ground containing water or mud

paralysed, paralysis – unable to move

parasites – organisms that live or feed off other animals and cause them harm

permeable – allows liquids or gases to pass through

pesticides – poisons used to kill animal pests

pet trade – the buying and selling of animals as pets

poach, poached – hunted illegally

pollinate, pollination – moving pollen from one flower to another to produce seed

pollinator – animals that pollinate plants

pollutants – substances that cause pollution

pores – small holes in the skin

postures – positions

poultry – chickens, ducks and geese, kept for their eggs and meat

predation – killing and feeding on other animals

predator, predators – animals that hunt and eat other animals

preen gland – an oil-producing body part near the tail

prehensile – able to grip

prey – animals caught by other animals and eaten

proboscis – a tube-like mouth for sucking, like an elephant's trunk

prod – to push gently

pupa – the non-feeding stage between the larva and adult stages in insects developing through complete metamorphosis

pupa, pupae – the non-feeding stage between the larva and adult stages in insects developing through complete metamorphosis

pupate, pupates – when a larva becomes a pupa

pupils – the round, black parts in the centre of eyes

purified – cleaned

raptor, raptors – birds of prey

rasping – a rough sound

recycle – to reuse

regurgitated – when food is brought back up from the stomach into the mouth

repel – to keep something away

reptiles – scaly, egg-laying, cold-blooded animals like crocodiles and lizards

resonance box – box in a musical instrument that makes sound loud, clear and strong

riverine – to do with rivers

rodents – small animals, such as rats and mice, that have constantly growing sharp front teeth

rudder, rudders – the steering part of a boat

rump – between the back and tail

saliva – liquid produced in the mouth; spit

sanitation – keeping things clean and healthy

sap – a watery fluid found inside plants

scavengers – animals that eat mainly dead animals

scent gland, scent glands – organs of the body that produce an animal's scent

scent trail – an invisible trail of scent that animals leave to attract or ward off other animals

secrete, secreted – to produce or make

segmented – separated into sections or parts

self-defence – ways of protecting yourself

shed – to cast off or lose

slender – thin

sluggish – slow-moving

snout – part of the head consisting of nose, jaws and surrounding area

sparse, sparsely – spread out

specialised – for a special use or purpose

sperm – the substance from a male that fertilises a female for reproduction

stampede – when animals in a group start running together in the same direction

stout – strong; thick

strain – to separate solids from liquid

streamlined – smooth movement; able to move through water easily

striking – attracting interest or attention because of some unusual feature

supplement – special substances you eat to keep you healthy

swamps – permanently waterlogged ground, often overgrown

swarm – a large group of animals moving together

talons – sharp claws or nails

tandem – lined up one behind the other, facing the same direction

tentacles – long, narrow, flexible organs usually used for feeding, feeling or grasping

termitaria – mounds built by some termite colonies

territorial – when animals protect their territories from other animals of the same species

territory, territories – the area defended by an animal to keep other animals of the same species out

thermals – rising air currents; warm air moving upwards

thorax – the middle part of an invertebrate's body where the wings and legs are connected

toxic – poisonous

transparent – see-through

tufted – in clumps or bunches

urinate – get rid of urine from your body

urine – liquid waste that is passed from an animal's body

venom – a liquid produced by some animals, which contains a poison

venomous – able to produce venom

vertebrae – the bones that make up the backbone

vibrations – tiny, repeated, shaking movements

wader, waders – a bird that walks through water

warren – the underground home of animals such as rabbits and suricates

wedge-shaped – thin at one side and thicker at the other

wetland – an area of land with water, like dams, ponds, lakes, rivers

References

African Insect Life. S.H. Skaife, J. Ledger & A. Bannister. 1979. Struik Publishers, Cape Town.

Beat about the Bush: Birds. Trevor Carnaby. 2008. Jacana Media, Johannesburg.

Beat about the Bush: Mammals. Trevor Carnaby. 2004. Jacana Media, Johannesburg.

Butterflies of Southern Africa: A Field Guide. Mark Williams. 1994. Southern Book Publishers, Halfway House.

Cape Town: The Cape Peninsula National Park and Winelands Discover the Magic. Jacana Media, Johannesburg. 1998.

Complete Guide to the Frogs of Southern Africa, A. Louis du Preez & Vincent Carruthers. 2009. Struik Nature, Cape Town.

Field Guide to Insects in the Kruger National Park. Leo Braack. 1991. Struik Publishers, Cape Town.

Field Guide to Insects of South Africa. 2nd Edition. Charles Griffiths, Mike Picker & Alan Weaving. 2004. Struik Publishers, Cape Town.

Field Guide to the Snakes and Other Reptiles of Southern Africa. Bill Branch. 1990. Struik Publishers, Cape Town.

Field Guide: Mammals of Southern Africa. Chris and Tilde Stuart. 1993. Struik Publishers, Cape Town.

Frogs and Frogging in Southern Africa. Vincent Carruthers. 2001. Struik Publishers, Cape Town.

Frogs of South Africa. Vincent A. Wager. 1986. Delta Books, Craighall.

Garden Route: From Still Bay to Storms River Discover the Magic. Jacana Media, Johannesburg. 2000.

Gauteng: Johannesburg, Pretoria & Beyond Discover the Magic. Jacana Media, Johannesburg. 2000.

Guide to the Reptiles of Southern Africa. A. Graham Alexander & Johan Marais. 2008. Struik Publishers, Cape Town.

KwaZulu-Natal: A Celebration of Biodiversity – Discover the Magic. Jacana Media, Johannesburg. 2001.

Mammals of Southern Africa. Deidre Richards. 1990. Struik Timmins Publishers, Cape Town.

Roberts Bird Guide: A comprehensive field guide to over 950 species in southern Africa. Hugh Chittenden. 2007. John Voelcker Bird Book Fund, Cape Town.

Roberts Birds of Southern Africa 7th edition. PAR Hockey, WRJ Dean & PG Ryan. 2006. John Voelcker Bird Book Fund, Cape Town.

Snakes and Other Reptiles of Southern Africa. Rod Patterson. 1991. Struik Publishers, Cape Town.

Southern Africa's Threatened Wildlife. John Ledger. 1990. Endangered Wildlife Trust, Johannesburg.

Southern African Spiders: An Identification Guide. Martin R. Filmer. 1995. Struik Publishers, Cape Town.

The Behaviour Guide to African Mammals. Richard Despard Estes. 1991. Russel Friedman Books, Halfway house.

The Eskom Red Data Book of Birds of South Africa, Lesotho and Swaziland. Keith. N. Barnes. 2000. BirdLife South Africa, Johannesburg.

The Mammals of the Southern African Subregion (new edition). J.D. Skinner and R.H.N. Smithers. 1990. University of Pretoria, Pretoria.

The Wildlife of Southern Africa: A Field Guide to the Animals and Plants of the Region. Vincent Carruthers. 1997. Southern Book Publishers, Johannesburg.

Tortoises, Terrapins and Turtles of Africa. Bill Branch. 2008. Struik Publishers, Cape Town.

Ulusaba Private Game Reserve Encountered. Jacana Media, Johannesburg. 1999.

What's that Snake? A Starter's Guide to Snakes of Southern Africa. Johan Marais. 2007. Struik Publishers, Cape Town.

Wild Ways: Field Guide to the Behaviour of Southern African Mammals. Peter Apps. 2000. Struik Publishers, Cape Town.

▶ Index

Page numbers in bold are the main entry for that species.

A

aardvark 17, 12, 33, 37, **61**, 215
aardwolf 7, **37**, 216
adder 194
  berg **194**
  gaboon 139, 145
  puff 139, 193, **194**
agama 171, 173, 180
  ground 180
  southern rock 138
  southern spiny 138, 140
  southern tree 134, 147, 180
ant **232**
  Argentine 233
  army 232
  cocktail 233
  pugnacious 233
antelope 15, 17, 20, 27, 33, 46, **49–53**, 55
  sable **51**
antlion 203, **217**
aphid **218**, 231, 233

B

baboon 7, 12, 20, 28, 55, 58, **59**, 127, 211
  chacma **59**
badger, honey **38**, 41, 135, 181, 193, 235
barbet **99**
  black-collared **99**
  crested **99**
bat 12, 30, **66–67**
  Cape serotine 66
  Egyptian free-tailed 66
  Egyptian fruit bat 67
  Wahlberg's epauletted fruit 67
Bateleur 76, 130
batis, Cape 84
bee 231, **234–235**
  carpenter 230, 236
  honeybee 231, 234

bee-eater 70, **107**
  little 107
  white-fronted 70, 107
beetles 42, 107, 111, 154, 168, 172, 180, 203, **222–227**, 230, 232, 238, 239, 257
  Addo flightless dung 224
  blister **226**
  Cape scarab 207
  dung 7, 204, **224**, 235
  giant longhorn 222
  longhorn 208
  rhinoceros 223
  rose 226
  whirligig 204, **223**
blowfly 230
boomslang 82, 147, **195**
buffalo 13, 23, 24, 27, **46**, 49, 60, 118, 169, 258
buffalo-weaver 102, **103**
  red-billed 103
bug, shield 218
bulbul **97**, 110
  Cape **97**
  dark-capped 72, 73, **97**
bullfrog 142, 156, **163**, 211
  giant **163**
bushbaby 14
  lesser 58
bushbuck 13, 49, **50**, 143
bushpig **60**
butterfly **239–243**
  Africa migrant 2441
  African monarch 242
  brown-veined white 241
  citrus swallowtail 242
  common opal 243
  Mooi River opal 243
  Brenton blue 206
  garden acraea 198
  mountain pride 199
  Table Mountain beauty 242
buzzard 124, **126**
  jackal 126
  steppe 126

C

caco, Boettger's **162**
canary, Cape 94
caracal 26, 30, **31**, 57, 63, 71
cat, African wild 26, **31**
centipede 100, **249**, 254
chameleon 135, 143, 149, 164, 171, 173, **176**, 195
  Cape dwarf 177
  Drakensberg dwarf 177
  flap-neck 135, 176, 199
  Natal Midlands dwarf 177
cheetah 12, **18**, 21, 22, 26, 27, **29**, 36, 54
chicken 81
cicada **219**
civet, African 12, **40**, 249
cobra **193**
  Cape 193
  Mozambique spitting 193
coot, red-knobbed **122**
cormorant 117, **121**
  reed 121
crane 86, **93**
  blue 93
  grey crowned 93
  wattled 93
cricket 172, 200, **29–211**, 255
  common 201, 202, **210**
  king 108, **210**
crocodile, Nile 92, **182**
crow 74, 85, 94, 106, 117
cuckoo 84, **110**
  Diderick 110
  Jacobin 110
  red-chested 110

D

damselfly 212, 213
darter, African 117, **121**
dassie **57**, 127, 128, 135, 187
dove, laughing 96
dragonfly 154, 213
drongo 106
  fork-tailed 106

square-tailed 77, 106
duck 80, 81, 94, 115, **120**, 121, 122
    yellow-billed 120
duiker 13, 55
    blue 55
    common 10, 55
    red 55

E

earthworm 108, 172, 190, 198, 246, 247, **248**, 249
    giant 248
eagles 55, 57, 58, 80, 81, 89, 94, 106, 117, 124, **127**
    African crowned 127
    martial 127
    tawny 81, 124
    Verreaux's 129
eagle-owl 89, 92
    spotted 76, 129
    Verreaux's 129
egg-eater **189**
    common 149, **189**
egret 81, 116, 117, **118**, 123
    cattle 115, 118
    great 118
    little 118
eland **49**
elephant, African 67, 13, 15, 20, 21, 23, 24, **43**, 60
elephant-shrew **62**
    four-toed 62

F

fiscal, common 98
fish-eagle 115
    African 128
flies **228–229**
    bee 228
    robber 230
francolin 88, **90**
    crested 71
    grey-winged 90
frogs 31, 39, 40, 60, 62, 98, 100, 109, 115, 116, 119, 121, 124, 126, **134–150**, 142, **152–163**

arum lily **160**
    banded rubber 144
    bushveld rain 141, 144
    Cape Peninsula moss 158
    Cape river 155
    Cape sand 157
    common platanna 139, 142, **154**
    common river 155
    foam nest 144, **161**
    greater leaf-folding 161
    micro **162**
    Mozambique rain 159
    Natal chirping 158
    Natal sand 157
    Natal tree 146
    painted reed 160
    plain rain 159
    Table Mountain ghost 150
    tinker reed 146

G

gecko 100, 135, 149, 171, 173, **178–179**, 255
    Cape dwarf 179
    marbled African leaf-toed 179
    Moreau's tropical house 178, 179
    Van Son's 171
gemsbok 17, 51
genet **40**, 65, 135, 188
    large-spotted 40
    small-spotted 40
giraffe 6, 13, 15, 27, **47**, 49, 258
goose 94, 115, **120–121**
    Egyptian 120
go-away-bird, grey 112
grassbird, Cape 85
grasshopper 42, 71, 172, 202, **209–211**
    bladder 205, 211
    elegant 205, 211
ground-hornbill **109**
    southern 109
guineafowl 81, 88, **89**
    crested 89
    helmeted 89

H

hare, scrub 63
Hamerkop 123
hartebeest 28, **52**
    red 52
helmet-shrike, white-crested 96
herald, red-lipped 191
heron 81, **116**, 117, 118, 119, 122, 123
    black-headed 116
    goliath 116
    grey 116
hippo **45**, 169
hoopoe **100**
    African 100
hornbill **109**
    crowned 109
    trumpeter 109
hyena 7, 28, **34–35**, 36, 54, 61, 131, 166
    brown 34
    spotted 34, 38
hyrax, rock see dassie

I

ibis **108**
    hadeda 108
    sacred 108
impala 13, 19, 28, 29, 32, **54**, 131, 187

J

jacana, African 78, 115
jackal 12, **33**, 41, 63, 65, 86, 131, 135, 166, 173
    black-backed 12, 30, 33

K

katydid, grass 209
kingfisher **105**, 116
    brown-hooded 105
    giant 105
    pied 105
kite **125**
    black-shouldered 125
    yellow-billed 125

klipspringer **19**, 56
kudu 13, 49, 50

L
ladybird 218
lapwing **91**
  blacksmith 91
  crowned 91
leguaan, *see* monitor lizard
leopard 9, 12, 14, 20, 21, **26**,
  27, 28, 36, 38, 57, 58, 65,
  88, 97, 131, 135
lion 6, 7, 8, 9, 12, 14, 21, 24,
  26, 27, 33, 35, 36, 39, 46,
  47, 54,131
lizard
  armadillo girdled 145
  Cape crag 174
  Drakensberg crag 175
  giant plated 174
  tropical girdled 171
  Warren's girdled 175
  yellow-throated plated 141

M
mamba **192**
  black 192
  green 192
mantis, praying 199, 202,
  205, **220**
martin **114**
  rock 114
masked-weaver, southern
  103
millipede **249**, 254
molerat, common **64**
monitor lizard 150, 166, 171,
  173, **181**, 185
  rock 181
  water 181
mongooses **41**, 65, 88, 135,
  166, 190, 193
  banded 42
  dwarf 42, 216
  slender 41
  yellow 41
monkey 12, 28, **58–59**, 127,
  187, 237, 249

samango 15
  vervet 20, 21, 59
moorhen 122
mosquitoes 67, 71, 135,
  154, 179, 199, 213, 219,
  228–229
moths 107, 146, 200, 230,
  231, **239–245**
  convolvulus hawk 245
  cream-striped owl 245
  emperor 239
  hawk 207
  horn 244
mouse **65**
  striped 65, 125
  grey climbing 65

N
nyala 13, 49, **50**
nightjar, fiery-necked 82

O
oribi **10**, 56
ostrich 77, **88**, 94
otter **39**
  African clawless 39
  spotted-necked 39
owls 57, 81, 94, 97, 124, 129

P
padloper (tortoise) **168**
  parrot-beaked 168
  speckled 168
pangolin 7, 12, 17, **61**
paradise-flycatcher, African
  106
parrot 5, 111, **113**
  brown-headed 113
  Cape 113
pelican, great white 80
penguin 77
pigeon **95**, 96
  African green 95
  speckled 95
platanna 139, 142, **154**
plover, three-banded 123
polecat, striped 6, **38**

porcupine **17**, 20, 33, 37, 47,
  61, 65
puffback, black-backed **96**
python 55, 143, 150, 181,
  187
  southern African 187

Q
quelea, red-billed 82

R
rabbits 20, 25, 28, 31, 33, **63**
  riverine 25
  Smith's red rock 63
rat, vlei 65
reedbuck 28, 29, 32, 53
rhino 13, 25, **44**, 60
  black 13, 25, 44
  white 13, 22, 25, 44
rinkhals 145
robin-chat, Cape 110
roller, lilac-breasted 71

S
sandgrouse, double-banded
  88
sandpiper, wood 123
scorpions 38, 190, 198, 200,
  202, **254–257**
  Cape burrowing 254
  shiny burrowing 255
  tailless whip 257
  Transvaal thick-tailed 256
  Zulu flat rock serval 255
  Water 219
serval 30
shrew **62**
  forest 62
shrike, see helmet-shrike
skaapsteker, spotted **191**
skinks 149, 171, **172**
  Cape 172, 173
  dwarf burrowing 173
  eastern striped 173
  legless 172
  rainbow 173
slug 86, 142, 210, **246**, 257

slug-eater **190**
    common 190
snails 108, 122, 142, 163, 168, 181, 190, 198, 210, **247**
    giant land 247
snakes 38, 42, 57, 61, 88, 97, 103, 117, 124, 126, 135, 136, 140, 143, 145, 147, 149, 164, 171, 172, 181, **184–195**, 256
    brown house 186, 188
    common brown water 135
    Eastern tiger 185
    harlequin 190
    mole 189
    Namib sand 185
    olive grass 184
    red-lipped herald 191
    spotted house 186
    vine 195
    worm 190
sparrow 74, 80, 81, 110, Cape **94**
spiders 98, 106, 142, 172, 190, 200, 202, 246, **250–253**
    baboon **253**
    bark 251
    fishing 253
    golden orb-web 250, 251
spoonbill, African 117
springbok 16, 28, 29, 32
spurfowl **90**
    Natal 90
    Swainson's 90
squirrel 18, **64**, 192
    ground 18
    tree 64
starling 31, 85, **101**
    Cape glossy 101, 111
    red-winged 101
steenbok 56
stick insect 202, **221**

stilt, black-winged 78
storks **119**, 123
    marabou 115, 119
    saddle-billed 74, 119
    white 74
    yellow-billed 115
suni 56
sugarbird, Cape 71
sunbird 104, 110
    malachite 104
    southern double-collared 104
    white-bellied 104
sun spider 257
suricate 41
swallow **114**
    barn 79
    blue 86, 114
    lesser-striped 114

T
termites 7, 37, 61, 91, 172, 179, 180, 190, 202, **214–216**, 257
    common 216
    harvester 7, 216
terrapin 136, 149, **165–170**
    marsh 169
    serrated hinged 169
thick-knee **92**
    spotted 80, 92
    water 92
tick 46, 59, 60, 71, 169, 202, **258–259**
    heartwater 258
toads 139, 144, 148, 152, 154, **156**, 157, 163
    guttural 142, 153, **156**
    raucous 153, 156
    red 136, 137
    western leopard 156
tortoises 35, 124, 143, **165–169**, 181
    angulate 138, 166, 167
    geometric **151**
    leopard 166
    Natal hinged 168

parrot-beaked padloper 168
    speckled padloper 168
turaco **112**
    Knysna 112
    purple-crested 112
turtle, leatherback 165
turtle-dove, Cape 96
twinspot, pink-throated 80

V
vultures 33, 86, 103, 119, **130–131**
    bearded 86
    hooded 130
    lappet-faced 130
    white-backed 131
    white-headed 131

W
warthog 12, 46, 47, **60**, 61, 216, 258
wasps 107, 203, **231–238**
    fig 237
    paper 205, 238
    mason 238
    velvet ant 236
waterbuck 53
weaver, sociable 102
weevil 222
widowbird, long-tailed 83
wild dog 12, 23, 24, **32**, 36
wildebeest 13, 27, 28, 43, 48
    blue **52**
wood-hoopoe, green 100
woodpecker 81, 100, 101, **111**, 113
    cardinal 111
    ground 111
    Knysna 111

Z
zebra 7, 13, 16, 21, 23, 25, 27, 28, 43, 46, **48**, 183, 258
    Cape mountain 48
    plains (Burchell's) 48

First published by Jacana Media (Pty) Ltd
in 2011 as a box series
Published in this format in 2016

10 Orange Street, Sunnyside,
Auckland Park 2092, South Africa
+27 11 628 3200 | www.jacana.co.za

Cover photograph: Villiers Steyn
(www.shutterstock.com)

ISBN 978-1-4314-2329-3
Set in Helvetica 9.24/11.55pt
Printed and bound by Creda Communications
Job no. 002611